What Do We Know?

Observations of the Stange and Unusual

by

Arthur Machen

Darkly Bright Press

What Do We Know?
Observations of the Strange and Unusual
by
Arthur Machen

Introduction, notes, photos, supplementary material,
book design & layout:
© 2023 by Christopher Tompkins. *All rights reserved.*

Catalog Number 018

ISBN: 979-8-989944-1-0
Library of Congress Control Number: 2024931134

Publisher's Cataloging-in-Publication data

Names: Machen, Arthur, 1863-1947, author.
Title: What do we know? Observations of the strange and unusual / by Arthur Machen.
Description: Includes bibliographical references. | Cochiti Lake, NM: Darkly Bright Press, 2024.
Identifiers: LCCN: 2024931134 | ISBN: 979-8-989944-1-0
Subjects: LCSH Great Britain--Social life and customs. | Supernatural. | Essays. | BISAC LITERARY COLLECTIONS / European / English, Irish, Scottish, Welsh | LITERARY COLLECTIONS / Essays
Classification: LCC PR6025.A245 .W43 2024 | DDC 828/.91209--dc23

darkly bright
press · design

www.darklybrightpress.com

Contents

Introduction

For in a world of uncertainty this one thing is absolutely certain: that we have no real knowledge of any material thing whatsoever. The only real knowledge is of spiritual things, and that is in the possession of the saints, the poets, and the painters.

There are latent mysteries in all things, even in those which seem most devoid of mystery.

The more mysteries the better.

I

After rereading through the preceding excerpts, all of which are to be found in this little volume, it is tempting to halt work on this "introduction" and let the matter end there. Despite a strong desire to write about Machen, in the end, it seems quite clear that no one can really write anything about Machen better than he did.

Consider his books of memoirs—*Far Off Things, Things Near and Far* and *The London Adventure*. In each, he sets about to chart particular periods in his life, and while some of his activities and manner of living are explored, his struggles in both success and failure are discussed, the reader is equally confronted by gaps and silences. Major events are only vaguely referenced and even tragedies are veiled as well as the recoveries. And yet, even in the gaps, silence, and omissions, Machen speaks articulately.

This enchanting quality haunts the Welshman's fiction. In this collection, he elucidates the secret formula: "There is no explanation: very few writers have the courage to refuse explanations. Life is usually profuse in explaining away strange incidents, explaining away at the same time all their interest." While he sometimes failed to execute this precept, most of Machen's stories, strangely poetic and symbolically charged, leave us to ponder what he does not tell us.

The man is a mystery. If he was not, if he could be easily analyzed and catalogued, or labeled as this sort of writer or another, then I suppose my interest would have waned long ago and I might be concocting a different opener to another writer's work.

But, I am here. And so are you, the reader. We keep coming back, you and I. We continue to desire for the pleasant taste of mystery that Arthur Machen so artfully prepared for us.

This desire sends us into the wild places to search for more treasure. In fact, much of Machen's work still lies hidden in secret valleys. Even for a seasoned explorer, there seems always more to discover on that road that leads beyond the next hill. After cresting its summit, more valleys and peaks confront our eyes, each veiled by mist.

"Machen has gone and the mysteries remain." [1]

II

After a dozen years of beating the streets and wandering the countryside as a reporter for the *Evening News*, Arthur Machen left that paper under difficult circumstances in 1921. In fact, his entire tenure had been fraught with difficulty as he despised the profession with a deep horror of the soul. Doggedly, he persisted through the years of insult, discomfort, and famously, the hysterical episode of the "Bowmen," to prevent his family from suffering penury. Yet, almost fantastically, the gloom quickly dissipated for Machen as he experienced an unhoped-for occurrence.

Led by bibliophiles and intellectuals such as Vincent Starrett and Ben Hecht, Machen became the center of a vogue. Long overdue, he found acclaim as newly converted enthusiasts combed bookstalls and dealers for the rarest of items.

This renaissance, known as the "Machen Boom," initiated a great change in Machen's life and its significance for current admirers should not be underestimated. The upswell in interest for the writer's work encouraged publishers on both sides of the Atlantic to reissue volumes that in some cases had been out of print for decades. Furthermore, the demand for material allowed unpublished work to be brought into the light of day, such as Machen's Grail epic *The Secret Glory* published in 1922, but written fourteen years before. *Ornaments in Jade*, which had languished since 1897, was finally issued in a beautiful edition in 1924. Finally, the period helped encourage newly written material to flow from Machen's hand to be readily accepted by publishers. And while some of this new work fell short, such as *The Canning Wonder*—certainly his weakest book—what Machen reader today can imagine a world without *The London Adventure*?

In no small way, the "boom" of the first half of that decade helped ensure Machen's literary survival.

Personally, Machen, much accustomed to peaks and valleys, took the enthusiasm and attention in stride, but he couldn't help being affected. On February 12, 1924, he wrote to Munson Havens, an American correspondent:

"I have been busy during the last few weeks in an odd employment which is getting customary and common with me—signing sheets of limited editions of my books. First 1000 sheets of the 'Chronicle of Clemendy', an old, rare book of mine the Alexandrian Society of New York are reissuing. Then 1200 signatures for 'Ornaments in Jade,' which Knopf of New York is publishing sometime this spring. Last week I signed 200 copies of 'The London Adventure' to be issued by my London publisher, Martin Secker; and tomorrow I have 150 sheets of 'Dog & Duck' to attend to in the same fashion. So, on the whole, I am getting rather sick of the sight of my own signature..." [2]

However, all things come to an end, and by 1926, the frenzied interest in Machen's work had subsided. Despite a few brief upward ticks, his fame and reputation settled into a more modest position for the remainder of his life. While it lasted, the writer benefited financially to a humble degree, not only from the published books, but from sales of his manuscripts and personal copies to collectors. Yet, Machen claimed to have received little money from his books over his long career and there is no reason to doubt him. Despite the attention he received and the stacks of sheets he signed, Machen was far from financially secure throughout the twenties, the decade in which he entered his sixties.

To cope with this omnipresent situation, Machen continued to submit articles and reviews to a wide variety of periodicals. A brief listing will suffice to suggest the quantity of material he produced. During the years 1919-1923, Machen contributed twenty-seven articles to *The Lyons Mail*, and sixty-four items to *The London Graphic* in 1925 and 1926. In addition, he sold work to *T.P.'s and Cassell's Weekly*, *The Morning Post*, *John O'London's Weekly*, *The Sunday Express* and others.

Through these various and sundry means, Arthur Machen carved out his living with a pen.

III

Little is known about Machen's tenure at *The Observer*. For the moment, documentation is seemingly lacking about the events that led to his employment as a columnist with the periodical. In their biography of Machen, Reynolds and Charlton explain: "...it was a serious blow that his contract was not renewed."[3] So, here are the bare facts: Machen's column, "Queer Things," ran from March 14, 1926 to February 27, 1927 after which it was replaced with "Art and Artists" by Paul George Konody.

Yet, while it lasted, readers discovered delightful and curious investigations into the strange and the unusual every Sunday. "Queer Things" found a lively and interactive audience as Machen wrote of men disappearing without a trace, telepathically-induced stage fright, forgotten queer books, fairies gathering among the hills of Ireland, and of his own experience with a ghost. In particular, I find his discussion of "Dark Welshmen" illuminating with regard to some of my favorite stories. Much could be said about this and other topics, but he says it best, and I am not eager to fill up, and inadequately so, his chosen silences.

This volume collects forty-six of the forty-eight known installments of the column and is presented in chronological order. Reading through the pages, one is struck by the enormous sense of freedom Machen enjoyed while writing for the paper. Each segment is wonderfully *Machenalian* not only by subject, but in presentation.

Closing the collection is a two-part book review[4] by Machen and a published letter to the editor, all from the 1930s. A final article, "How London Lived in 1827," was published in the *Evening Standard* two months after his release from *The Observer*. It is Machen's only known contribution to the former newspaper. As with the previous volumes in this informal series, *A Reader of Curious Books* (2020) and *Mist and Mystery* (2022), this installment will grant Machen enthusiasts and scholars access to a body of fine work which has been largely inaccessible for nearly a century.

Finally, here is the queerest thing: *what do we know?* Machen asks this question time and time again. Paradoxically, it carries both his skepticism and his faith while ringing our ears as an echo from mysterious Llantrisant.

Christopher Tompkins

---

1 *There Are Some Who Mourn* (1948), p. 7.
2 *A Few Letters* (1932), p. 12-13.
3 *Arthur Machen, A Biography* (1963), p. 138.
4 *The Noble and Joyous Boke Entytled Le Morte D'Arthur, Volume I & II*

What Do We Know?

Observations of the Stange and Unusual

by

Arthur Machen

Darkly Bright Press

"QUEER THINGS."

BY ARTHUR MACHEN.

One

Among the queer books, one of the queerest that I have ever met is certainly "Le Moyen de Parvenir." I first came upon it in an odd way enough. About thirty-eight years ago I was a cataloguer in a second-hand—or "antiquarian"—bookseller's shop not far from Leicester-square. There was not much spare room in the place, so I did my work in a chamber underground, I suppose the original back-kitchen of the house before it went into business. And here, by perpetual gaslight, I viewed splendid and rare and exquisite books of all kinds; and tried to find interesting things to say about them in a brief space. And thus, in due time, a little dumpy, dim old book came before me: "Le Moyen de Parvenir."

It was a very early edition, perhaps the first. The title-page bore the date 1610. If I had stuck to my proper business, looked up the bibliographical authorities—there was a row of these before me, and I am glad to say that I have forgotten their very names long ago—and written a brief note as to the excessive rarity of the example, all would have been well. But I must needs dip into the book, to find out what it was about. I did not do that, for that is more than anyone has ever done or ever will do. Unfortunately I became interested as I read, and thus at last I came to translate "Le Moyen de Parvenir" into English. I was not mad, but oddity has often a fatal attraction for young people. They think more of the gargoyles grinning on the parapet than of the aspiration of the spire.

And what about the book, "Way to Attain" or "Way to Get On"? Well, it was written at the beginning of the seventeenth century by one François Béroalde de Verville, son of Matthieu Béroalde, a distinguished Renaissance scholar and Calvinist minister. The "de Verville" was added by the son in a purely decorative spirit. Much in the same way as, it is said, the Basque Honoré Balzac, taking the armorial bearings of the de Balzacs at the same time. François returned to the faith that his father had abandoned, took orders, and became a canon of the Cathedral Church of St. Gatien at Tours. He wrote many dull and improving books, which he signed, dabbled a good deal in Alchemy, and finally wrote "Le Moyen de Parvenir," which he did not sign. It was skeptical, contemptuous of Catholics and Huguenots alike, and full of "sculduddery"—to use an expressive Scots term: decidedly not the book for a canon to write. Evidently, they were stricter at Tours in the seventeenth century than we were at York in the eighteenth. Sterne was made a Prebendary for writing "Tristam Shandy," which is a "Moyen de Parvenir" plus genius. Instead, when I began to say something about "votre ancien chanoine, Béroalde de Verville" to the Archbishop of Tours in 1801, I found His Grace willing to avoid the subject.

But you would like to know what the book us about? Well, here is the beginning of it:—

For these things came to pass in the time, the era, the hegira, the olympiad, the year, the season, the month, the week, the day, the hour, the minute, and in the very second, when, through the progress and advice of the Demon of the Spheres, hard tennis balls gave place to soft, much to the prejudice of that noble antiquity which played so pleasantly. Confounded be all inventors of novelties, who corrupt youth, and trouble our play, without any regard for good manners.

And so forth, at considerable length, till we are last informed that Sophia, also called Madam, Wisest of the Wise, Pearl in the Sea of Science, Paragon of Perfection, but otherwise unidentified, had bidden the sages of the world to a banquet. The guests are named; a few of them are Socrates, Alexander the Great, Pythagoras, Rabelais, Beza, Caesear, Plotinus, Marot, Bacon, Erasmus, Zoroaster, and Aretino. As will be seen, all ages and all nations are represented, but there is not the faintest attempt to make the personages of the long dialogue—such is the scheme of the book, if it may be said to have a scheme—speak in character. For example, the following is not exactly Ciceronian in manner or matter, though Cicero is speaking:—

Hear this prophecy, which I learnt in the abbey of the caves of Memphis. "Monks, priests, ministers and the like, judges, barristers, and attorneys, and the like, merchants, mechanicals, craftsmen, and the like, of whatsoever sort or condition they be, who shall speak evil of these authentic memorials, styled the Way to Attain shall be attained and judged guilty of what crimes soever folly covers, impertinence hatches, and hypocrisy fosters."

It is true that there is a touch of his native soil about Buchanan (tutor to King James I.) when he says, "I would have you know that I am a gentleman, and, by the Blade and Handle, we are all gentlemen in my country." But, forthwith, he goes on to tell a good story about Louis XI., the Abbot of Turpenay, and Tristan l'Hermite, and Sappho and the famous Beza talk the tale over.

I suppose there are hundreds of tales in this monster of a book. Most of them are utterly gross, all are harmless, and a few are amusing. If you are in love with the queer for the sake of its queerness, read "Le Moyen de Parvenir"; otherwise let it abide on its dusty shelf.

Two

March 21, 1926

As a citizen of Caerleon-on-Usk, I am glad to hear that King Arthur's Round Table, otherwise the Roman Amphitheatre, is not to be industrialized. By the munificence of a great London paper this strange relic of the Roman world is to be preserved forever for the public good. Close at hand there is to be a noble power-station and beautiful housing accommodation for employees of the Newport Municipality: a pleasing juxtaposition of the new and the old.

I can remember Caerleon in the days of its peace, before great things were dreamed of. There was no railway. A slow chocolate and yellow omnibus trundled between "The Bull," Caerleon, and Newport Station, St. Julian's haunted wood being on the hillside above the river. They still talked of Tennyson's visit—when my grandfather, the Vicar, found the poet smoking a black clay pipe in his room at the fifteenth-century inn, "The Hanbury Arms." On New Year's Day the children followed the Roman custom of the *strenae (étrennes),* and carried round the gilded apples set with raisins and hazel nuts that seemed to grow from little twigs of box. And the bridge over the Soar brook was called Pont Sadwrn, which is Pons Saturni, and the village across the Usk was Caerleon ultra Pontem.

But the progressive spirit has been abroad in Caerleon for some time. When I was last there a magnificent red-brick lunatic asylum was a prominent feature of the landscape.

Mr. Howarth, the President of the Bolton Master Cotton Spinners' Association, is not content with the present fashions for ladies. He thinks that it is a mistake to go back to Eve for modes and roles. He hopes for a return to a saner way of dress, and to a Master Cotton Spinner a sane dress is a full dress, one for which much cotton is required.

Why not set the old dictum to work?

"What Lancashire thinks to-day, England will think to-morrow." Let Lancashire dream of fair women in flowing and ample robes; and we may wake up to romantic reality.

I see a new book announced! "Gilles de Rais, the original Bluebeard." Well; I don't believe it. Bluebeard was much more like Henry VIII. than Gilles de Rais, the knight who rode with St. Joan of Arc. The speciality of Bluebeard, as every well-regulated nursery knows, was wife-killing, a comparatively humane form of sport. But Gilles de Rais was a child-killer, and he killed children for the horrible ends of Black Magic. Horrible; though nonsensical. There is no such thing as Black Magic, certainly; but just as those who would be saints must exercise the heroic virtues, so those who would be Black Magicians must practice the diabolic vices: they must excel by far the measure of common human wickedness. As for Bluebeard, his is, no doubt, a very ancient folk-tale dating back far beyond the fifteenth-century.

There is a minor, though violent, dispute going amongst some trade unionists as to whether whitewash is paint or only whitewash. This particular whitewash is something more than common whitewash, it appears; there is bitumen in it. Wherefore, it is contended, it is really paint. And, certainly the painters of the old school used bitumen very freely when they wished to produce the effect of a landscape on which the arch-thunderstorm is about to fall. You remember Claude Lantier in "L'Oeuvre" on "the bituminous cookery of the academics"?

But every craft has these delicate distinctions. In the theatre, if the stage-cloth, the stuff laid down to cover the boards, is just a piece of neutral coloured material, then it is the business of the stage hands to lay it. But if it pretends to be a Turkish carpet or trim lawn, then it is the affair of the Property Man. I remember once, playing Tristan L'Hermite with George Alexander, making an exit with a lighted candle in my hand. I gave it to the first man I saw behind the scene, and he turned on me indignantly. "What do you mean by giving me that candle? Do you think I'm Props?" He was a stage-hand.

Covent Garden hates the thought of migrating to Bloomsbury. Bloomsbury, though already sadly fallen from the utter peace that used to dwell there, declares that a market in its midst will be its ruin; and the dwindling lovers of old London are sad at the thought, because they dislike all change. Old Convent Garden is a place of many memories. "Will's Coffee House," where Dryden reigned, was at the corner of Bow-street and Russell-street, on the western side. Will, otherwise William Urwin, once so far forgot himself as to threaten his boy, Thomas Parsons, who thereupon ran away. He wore, as the "London Gazette" stated, "an old Grey Serge Coat lined with black; an old pair of Trowsers, a black pair of stockings and black hat."

The ancient Gauls were *braccæ*, wore brecks, preferring the Oxford cut. But who would have suspected trousers in the seventeenth-century?

Some time ago I confessed that when I tarried in the precincts of the Tower, I always thought rather of Mrs. Quilp's tea party on Tower Hill than of Anne Boleyn or Lord Lovat. I advanced in explanation the theory that the great characters of Dickens are pure essences, whereas actual human beings are mixed; iron ore as compared with fine steel. I am confirmed in this view by the fact that a few days ago a certain illustrious personage in Dickens was twice referred to in strangely different circumstances. In the one case it was a question of an Elizabethan writer, Dekker, whose play, "The Black Rod and the White Rod," was sold at Sotheby's for £1,150. "He certainly was a Micawber," says the describer of the sale. The other instance deals with a Georgian bankrupt, a gentlemen who waited and hoped "for something good to turn up."

The Official Receiver: "Rather a Micawber attitude?"

The Bankrupt: "Yes."

I estimate that Mr. Micawber was born somewhere about 1785. How many people born much later are as alive as he to-day?

Three

March 28, 1926

We all know that the man who has no music on his soul is fit for treasons, stratagems, and spoils. But is there such a thing as having rather too much music in one's soul? The other day a gentleman wrote to the paper to tell us exactly how he felt about music. He dislikes most of the older composers: detests Bach, is left cold by Beethoven, abominates the "Messiah," and is made furiously angry by Mozart and Verdi—odd companions, by the way. On the other hand, Vaughn Williams moves him to such an extent, "that sometimes I feel I can bear it no longer; Holst excites me so much that I could stand up and shout for joy; Elgar has many times moved me to the verge of tears."

And I cannot help being reminded of Boswell on "the power of musick." "I told him [Johnson] that it affected me to such a degree, as often to agitate my nerves painfully, producing in my mind alternate sensations of pathetick dejection, so that I was ready to shed tears; and of daring resolution, so that I was inclined to rush into the thickest part of the battle."

"Sir," (said he), "I should never bear it, if it made me such a fool."

Dr. Armitage Robinson, Dean of Wells, has attacked a very pretty problem in his "Two Glastonbury Legends," to be published by the Cambridge University Press. He inquires whether any historical truth underlies the legends connecting Glastonbury with St. Joseph of Arimathea, the Holy Grail, and the Arthurian legend. Well, to the best of my belief, William of Malmesbury, writing about 1130, is the first person to connect St. Joseph with Glastonbury. William says that the body of St. Joseph is buried in the abbey precinct; also that two phials containing the Precious Blood, are buried in the saint's tomb.

The story is, therefore, a late one. The sixth century British writers make no mention of Glastonbury or of St. Joseph of Arimathea. Indeed, one of them declares expressly that nothing is known of the first evangelists of Britain. But I have always believed that William of Malmesbury's statement bore an important part in the shaping of the Grail Romances. There seems little doubt that the Celtic Grail was a portable altar. It remains an altar—"the Stone from Heaven"—in the Parsifal of Wolfram von Eschenbach. The phials of William of Malmesbury are the first hint of the final form taken by the Grail—the Chalice.

We are always learning. I have been getting a good deal of fresh light lately on certain well-known characters. These characters are the Giant (or Ogre), Daddy, and the Boy. A gentleman whose name I cannot recollect (though he is evidently a most advanced thinker), says that a father should never criticise, much less punish his son. It is the neglect of this precept, he declares, that has led to the well-known and unhappy result that the Boy always identifies The Giant or Ogre, or any other harsh and villainous personage of the fairy tales with Daddy. And then there is a lady, who approaches the matter from a somewhat different standpoint. She says that children should never read fairy tales, because the little ones always sympathise with the Ogre (or Giant), and thus become exactly like Giants (or Ogres) in after life. Who would have thought it?

And I also gather from *The Observer* of last Sunday the information that a man of considerable reading has written a book showing that Bacon wrote "Don Quixote" and Montaigne's "Essays," as well as Shakespeare's plays. I do not know why I place this statement beside the doctrines concerning Daddy and the Giants. But I feel that, somehow, there is a mysterious link between all three.

I have been reading of the case, a well authenticated one, as I believe, of the cat who was taken from Godalming to Leeds, and found its way back to its old home two months later. How is this done? The cat was, no doubt, shut up in a basket, taken by train to Waterloo, driven across London, and then entrained for Leeds; by what imaginable sense could it re-thread this track which it has not even seen?

But there are many mysteries in the world of animals. Why does a moth seek the candle flame? One scientific authority says that the moth sees the candle as the end of a tunnel, as an escape into the light. But, the candle apart, the moth dreads the light and avoids it. Another naturalist told me that the moth takes the candle for a flower. But it will return again and again after it has been singed; surely it would not continue to see nourishment from a consuming flame? My own explanation has no scientific nonsense about it: the moth seeks in the candle fire a world of glory, beauty, and delight, and is not to be held back, even by the pains of burning; thus prefiguring the nature of man.

And, by the way, the only ghost story that I can tell at first hand relates to an animal, a favourite cat. Tom, the well-beloved, had been the prop of the house for sixteen years and more. At last he dies, full of years and honour. The day after, in the evening, we sat by the fire and thought of the empty chair. Suddenly, the crumpled papers in and about the wastepaper basket were violently and audibly agitated. I went to the spot, thinking we had a rat for a visitor. The papers were all still; there was nothing there. And, a minute or two later, there came a very familiar sound: the soft thump of a cat's feet falling on the carpet, as it jumps from a slight height into a room. "Ah," said I, "that must be the cat from next door." I went to the window, thinking that the lower part must be open slightly at the top, since it was a cold April night. It was, I think, a week later that my wife and I heard the well-remembered sound of Tom's bell ringing on the lawn. There was no other bell-bearing cat resident in the neighbourhood, and we never heard the bell again.

Forty years ago I was travelling back from Brighton with a cheerful Bank Holiday crowd. We passed a plantation of willows in full catkin, and there was a cry of "Look at the palms." Country-bred, I had never heard willows called palms before, and have often wondered why the cockney never calls them anything else. No doubt, they were used in the Middle Ages as a substitute for palm branches in the ceremonies of Palm Sunday. But these ceremonies disappeared with Queen Mary; a long time ago. Still, tradition and custom endure long in England. I believe that down in Devonshire people carried bunches of willow or posies of flowers to church on Palm Sunday in quite recent times.

Four

April 4, 1926

Let us hope that the new Memorial Theatre at Stratford-on-Avon will be a worthier monument than the old. The burnt theatre was, most certainly, one of the queerest things that I have ever seen; whether considered externally or internally. Architecturally, it was a mixture of several styles. The ground floor was in what I shall take leave to call Protestant Sunday School Gothic. The pepper-pot treatment of the tower suggested—faintly—a French château. The roof belonged to a German town-hall.

Inside, and considered practically, it was queerer still. The stage was on the first floor, so that all the scenic apparatus had to be hoisted up by some rope and pulley contraption of a nautical character. Though designed in the first place for Shakespearean performances, that is, for large companies, there were, I think, only five dressing-rooms. In these, the principals dressed; the rest of the company made the best of certain gloomy vaults the level of the Avon. But nobody grumbled or wanted to grumble. Actors enjoy discomforts. In my own short stage career I dressed in a petrol shed, a disused coach-house, a Sixth Form room, Marlborough Police Court, in a greenhouse (in July), and behind a haystack—and I loved them all.

I saw an odd definition of necromancy the other day. A writer in a well-known Spiritualist journal said that it meant divination by corpses. Of course νεκρός means both a corpse and a dead man's spirit; but it is to the latter sense that necromancy has signified, the evocation of the spirits of the dead, and the conversing with them. In the Middle Ages, the world was sometimes spelt "nigromancy": a kind of early Hobson-Jobson, emphasising the blackness of the Black Art.

"Body" and "corpse" are words that are often confused. A clergyman, an old friend of mine, once told that he wished he had the courage to begin a discourse on certain deep matter of theology with the words of Mr. Mantalini: "I will be a body—a dead, damp, moist, unpleasant body." "Then," said the cleric, "I should continue: Mr. Mantalini was speaking loosely. He was a body. He meant, 'I will be a corpse'—a totally different thing."

...

Last Sunday a correspondent of *The Observer* permitted himself to use language which I must call revolutionary. He actually requested the Prime Minister to reflect that a nation does not live by coal alone. He was thinking of Canterbury, the city that is thirteen hundred years old, the true metropolis of England, a place of deep peace, and beauty, and lovely and splendid memories! They are going to ring it about with collieries, and that necessary adjunct to collieries, colliers' dwelling. Well, why not? Caerleon, the legionary and legendary city, has its great lunatic asylum, and will soon have its great power station. It is idle to attempt to stay the wheel of progress; and so Waterloo Bridge will soon be broken down. The Florentines do not seem to understand the spirit of the age. The municipality proposed to pull down some ancient houses and build an arcade almost as nice as the arcade at Brixton. But there was a fuss, and it is now suggested that it is the municipality, and not the old houses, that will have to go.

One morning in Fleet-street an old gentleman with whom I was slightly acquainted hailed me as I got off my bus. I did not recognise him for a moment, and he went on: "I don't think you remember me?" Recognition came, and I replied, crossly: "Oh, yes, I do. You are the man who pulled down Dr. Johnson's house." I am not sure whether this was the house in Johnson's-court, or No. 8, Bolt-court, where the doctor died.

Last year, travelling down in Kent, a great charabanc, full of trippers, passed us on the road. It was called, oddly, "Timpson's Blue-Eyed Maid." And a few days ago I read that a fleet of omnibuses, called Timpson's Silver Omnibuses, plying to the South-eastern suburbs, have been transferred to another firm. These statements may seem insignificant; but they are far from being so to the true Dickensian. "When I departed from Dullborough (? Rochester) in the strawy arms of Timpson's Blue-Eyed Maid, Timpson's was a moderate-sized coach-office (in fact, a little couch-office), with an oval transparency in the window, which looked beautiful by night, representing one of Timpson's coaches in the act of passing a milestone on the London road with great veracity, completely full inside and out, and all the passengers dressed in the first style of fashion, and found no such place as Timpson's now. ... Pickford had come and knocked Timpson's down."

Thus Dickens in "Dullborough Town." I think he would be glad to know that Timpson still flourishes, in spite of all. And the passengers on the Blue-Eyed Maid which I saw last year certainly appeared to be enjoying themselves tremendously.

A copy of a rare book, by Dr. Dee, was sold by auction recently. Dr. Dee was a man of science and a man of magic, too; the combination was unusual enough in the Elizabethan age in which he lived. The British Museum, I believe, possesses his famous "crystal" or "Devil's Looking-glass," which, in fact, is a piece of cannel coal.

It is not on record that anyone has seen anything of the least consequence in any crystal—which in the East is often a small pool of ink poured into the scryer's hand. But there is no doubt as to the existence of the phenomenon. If people of a certain habit and constitution look long enough into a bright surface they will see things as surely as other people will see things—if they drink enough brandy. Seeing is by no means believing. A country doctor gave a patient medicine containing belladonna—and the patient saw a black hen sitting on the top of the grandfather clock. The doctor stopped the belladonna, and the fowl vanished. Later, the patient said: "I suppose that I must believe now that there was no hen on the clock. But I can scarcely believe it, because I saw the hen with my own eyes."

Queer Things

Five

April 11, 1926

Six hundred people have recently been climbing the Pillar Rock, in Cumberland. I have seen photographs of the climb, and the mere photographs make me experience a certain sinking feeling. You see a figure pressed against the sheer precipice, the feet balanced on a nine-inch projection, the hands clasping the rock; dread height above and dread depth below. And these people do this for fun; because they like it.

From any rationalistic, or even rational point of view, it is evident that they are guilty of the craziest folly. And it is probable that this very fact, that man delights at times in crazy follies, differentiates him from the brutes. He is addicted to poetry, martyrdom, and rock climbing; to pursuits which have never been so much as contemplated by the most learned pig.

The Harwich Tunnel hoax seems dull. Hundreds of motorists received invitations to be present at the opening of a submarine tunnel between Harwich and Felixstowe. A good many of them turned up—and there was no tunnel. Some of the motorists laughed, others were cross; there seems but small flavour in the jest. The best practical joke, I have always thought, was that played by Toole on the Bancrofts. Mr. and Mrs. Bancroft, as they were then, were enjoying an excellent lunch at a smart Parisian restaurant. Suddenly, the attention bestowed on them, which had been excellent, became magnificent. The proprietor took the place of the maitre d'hotel. Exquisite meats, the rarest drinks were pressed on them. The bill was enormous; but the whole establishment bowed low when they went out.

Toole, latent at a remote table, had seen the Bancrofts come in. He had whispered in the restaurant management that they were members of the English Royal Family, travelling in strict incognito.

The Observer Telepathic Competition interests me, though I have not ventured to send in my own experience. It was thus: I was playing a very small part in "If I Were King" at the St. James's Theatre.[1] There

---

1 See page 30 for excerpts from the program for this play.

were four or five of us depicting certain minor villains. In the old days we should have been called "Responsibles," because, I suppose, the responsibility attaching to the parts was so very small. But we had our little scene. One after the other was summoned before the saviour of France, the transfigured Villon, and one after the other had his chance of "standing out" for a moment. I had done my bit, and had said all I had to say for the rest of the play; my "responsibility" was over. Another ruffian succeeded me, and as he began, to my amazement, I was seized with stage-fright in its most horrid form. And I was just beginning to ask myself what I meant by it when my successor "dried: dead." He stood speechless in the centre of the stage. I have always believed that his terror was communicated to me. I had no cause for fright.

With humility, I stand corrected in the matter of the Moth and the Flame. A correspondent of *The Observer* assures me that I am mistaken in supposing that the moth seeks in the candle flame a world of glory and delight. He says that the flame acts as a directive stimulus, and that the response of the insect is a tactic tropism. There is always something appealing in scientific explanations. I never knew why leaves were green till I read in some good book that the green colour was due to the presence of chlorophyll in the leaves. Chlorophyll means "green leafiness." And I once remarked to a doctor that I understood that asparagus was a very wholesome vegetable. "Is that so?" said he. "Well, it must be due to the presence of "asparagine." "Asparagine" signifies, I suppose asparagusness. There is a distinct flavour of the Scholastic Philosophy about these explanations. I am reminded of Martinus Scriblerus, who showed that a meatjack roasted meat because it possessed an inherent meat-roasting property.

Let us still be scientific. I was saying quite recently how the dietetic whirligig had brought in his revenges in the case of Mr. Squeers, the schoolmaster. Mr. Squeers, it may be remembered, got into trouble over his treatment of a delicate pupil. He explained that when a boy failed to fancy his food he was sent "grazing"—turned into a neighbour's turnip-field and invited to eat as many turnips as he liked. If it were a delicate case, Mr. Squeers added, the turnip field was alternated with a carrot patch.

It has long been known, of course, in Food Reform circles, that cooking ruins the value of everything, and that raw vegetables constitute an absolutely ideal diet; but I was delighted to see only last week an emphatic testimony to Mr. Squeers's enlightened theories from Sir W. Arbuthnot Lane. This distinguished surgeon, writing on the gross neglect of the health of schoolboys and schoolgirls, says: "The only schoolmaster who I ever heard of who attended systematically to the health of the children under his care was the much-reviled Mr. Squeers, and he has been held up to ridicule and contempt in consequence."

"Nicholas Nickleby" is, I am afraid, rather an old-fashioned book, so perhaps Food Reformers, parents, schoolmasters, and schoolmistresses, may be glad to have an outline of the Squeers Diet. In the morning, brimstone and treacle were given. This was followed by Breakfast, consisting of porridge, looking like diluted pincushions without the covers. To this succeeded a minute wedge of bread—brown, of course. Dinner was of three courses:—

Stirabout
or
Cow's Liver Broth.
Potatoes.
Salt Beef.

The salt beef was cut from the bodies of horned cattle who had died a natural death; Mr. Squeers being opposed to cruelty to animals. Supper was of bread and cheese; cheese is a highly concentrated food. The treatment followed in the case of delicate boys has already been indicated.

A recent article on Pins and the superstitions connected with these prickly and harassing objects mentions their use in sorcery; their insertion in the waxen or clay man, who was the image of the enemy to be destroyed by the witch. Some thirty or forty years ago a Somersetshire folk-lorist came upon such images, hidden in chimney nooks and crannies. He mentions a certain peculiarity in the fashioning of the figures. About a hundred and sixty years ago an Italian which showed the adventurer, Casanova, an image which she had made for his torture and death. The recipe for the figure was the same in Italy as it was in Somerset in the 'eighties of the last century; and perhaps the witches of the Stone Age knew no other way.

ST. JAMES'S THEATRE.

Sole Lessee and Manager ... ... Mr. GEORGE ALEXANDER

Produced on Saturday Evening, August 30th, 1902.

TO-DAY at 2, and EVERY EVENING at 8 o'clock,

Will be Acted a Romantic Play, in Four Acts, entitled

IF I WERE KING

By JUSTIN HUNTLY McCARTHY.

François Villon	Mr. GEORGE ALEXANDER
Louis XI. (*King of France*)	Mr. CHARLES FULTON
Tristan L'Hermite (*Provost of Paris*)	Mr. ALFRED BRYDONE
Olivier le Dain (*the King's Barber*)	Mr. E. VIVIAN REYNOLDS
Thibaut d'Aussigny (*Grand Constable of France*) ...	Mr. E. LYALL SWETE
Noel le Jolys (*a Courtier*)	Mr. HENRY AINLEY
René de Montigny	Mr. HERBERT DANSEY
Guy Tabarie	Mr. W. R. STAVELEY
Colin de Cayeulx }... ... (*Friends of Villon*)	Mr. H. CARTER BLIGH
Jehan le Loup	Mr. ARTHUR MACHEN
Casin Cholet	Mr. G. A. SEAGER
Robin Turgis (*an Innkeeper*)	Mr. RICHARD DALTON
Trois Echelles }	Mr. PERCY JACKSON
Petit Jean } ... ... (*Hangmen*) ...	Mr. C. LINDLEY
Du Lau	Mr. GREGORY SCOTT
Poncet de Rivière }... (*French Knights*)	Mr. REGINALD DANE
De Nantoillet	Mr. STUART DENNISON
Toison d'Or (*the Burgundian Herald*)	Mr. ERNEST GRIFFIN
Montjoye (*the French Herald*)	Mr. H. R. HIGNETT
An Astrologer	Mr. B. FAIRCLOUGH
Captain of the Watch	Mr. F. HENDERSON
Katherine de Vaucelles	Miss JULIE OPP
Huguette du Hamel	Miss SUZANNE SHELDON
Jehanneton la Belle Heaulmière	Miss AURIOL LEE
Blanche	Miss MAY SAKER
Guillemette ... ... (*Companions of Huguette*)	Miss DOROTHY SCOTT
Isabeau	Miss JEAN MACKINLAY
Denise	Miss BEATRICE BECKLEY
Mother Villon	Miss BESSIE PAGE
The Queen	Miss MURIEL MYLES

Ladies, Courtiers, Knights, Monks, Archers, Soldiers, Citizens, Peasants, Bohemian Gipsy Dancers, Torchbearers, Attendants, Pages, &c.

Matinees : Every Wedne:

HÔTEL AND RESTAURANT DIEUDONNÉ, ONE MINUTE'S WAI

René de Montigny	Mr. HERBERT DANSEY
Guy Tabarie	Mr. W. R. STAVELEY
Colin de Cayeulx }... ... (*Friends of Villon*) ...	Mr. H. CARTER BLIGH
Jehan le Loup	Mr. ARTHUR MACHEN
Casin Cholet	Mr. G. A. SEAGER

Excerpts from original program:
Collection of the Editor.

Six

April 18, 1926

There have been complaints lately about the brevity of modern theatrical entertainment. One critic says that going to the play now is like being asked to dinner and being given instead three delicious cocktails—with intervals between them. Certainly, the bill of the play now is like the bill of fare; not so solid as it used to be.

There is an old playbill before me; and yet not such a very old playbill, the date, December 5, 1870. The theatre is the Princess's, and, the management consisted of Benjamin Webster and F. B. Chatterton. Well, on Monday, December 5—Cattle Show Week—the show began at 7:00 p.m. with the Irish Romantic Drama, "Peep o' Day." In the cast, I noticed the names of W. Rignold, Shell Barry, and Miss Rose Leclercq. At 8:45, "Peep o' Day" was succeeded by the celebrated Military Vaudeville, "Pretty Girls of Stilberg"; in the cast, Mr. Benjamin Webster and Mr. John Clayton. There was a great scene: "Review of the Female Warriors! Commander in Chief, Miss Rose Leclercq." and the entertainment concluded with the farce: "He's a Lunatic." And I am sure that the audience sat through it all and enjoyed it immensely. They were brave days.

An ancient drinking vessel has just been found at Northfleet, Kent. It was discovered lying near a human skeleton, and it is remarked that this circumstance dates the period of internment, since, Christianity being recognized officially in 330 A. D., from that time the burial of various articles with the dead ceased.

And here I seem to see one of the many difficulties in writing history. I was talking not long ago with a man who was brought up in a Northamptonshire village, partly agricultural, partly industrial in his employment. He told me how one of the village lads died of consumption. "The poor chap used to be very fond of tinned salmon, so his relations put a tin of salmon in the coffin. After the funeral was over, they recollected that they had forgotten the tin opener, and they were a great deal put out about it. But as it happened, a cousin, a girl, died a couple of months afterwards, and as the two had been great friends, the family put the tin opener in her coffin, and everybody said it would be all right." This must have happened about 1875-85. In the same village the local builder gave particular directions as to the position of his grave in the churchyard. He chose a place whence he could see a row of cottages which he had run up soon before he died.

"The Pagan custom of burying various articles with the dead was discontinued after 330 A. D." And here you have the Pagan custom flourishing in the Northampton village of forty, fifty years ago. And for all I know, it flourishes to this day.

The critics have been finding fault with the players' accents in "Hell-Bent for Heaven." One of them said that the actors vacillated between the dialect of Derbyshire and Devonshire, the scene being the mountains of North Carolina. I consulted an American friend as to this matter, and he advised me that it was generally safe to drawl when playing a Southern part. But the stage has always been a little lax in this matter of accent. Not long ago, a friend of mine was asked to undertake the part of a Sussex countryman. "But," said he, "I don't know anything about the Sussex dialect." The manager smiled benignly, and inquired, "What's the matter with good old Loamshire?"

The Earl of Bessborough, addressing the touring Hotel Owners, made a grievance of the fact that the modern hotel-keepers occupy the same position before the law as their predecessors, the innkeepers, did 300 years ago. Even to-day, he remarked, disputes were dealt with in the law courts in accordance with a legal decision arrived at in 1584. That might sound incredible to the visitors—the visitors had laughed—but it was true, and it was incredible in face of the contrast between the inn of 300 years ago and the modern hotel.

Yet, I am sure that there was very snug lying at the Tabard in Southwark five hundred years ago. And as to three hundred years ago:—

"And whereas through time it hath been much decaied, it is now by Master J. Preston, with the Abbots house: Thereto adjoyned, newly repaired, and with convenient rooms much encreased, for the receipt of many guests."

The Tabard was, in fact, replete with every modern luxury and convenience: as such things were understood in the year 1598.

The Salmon and the Torch may be sighted as a companion to the Moth and the Flame. When Sir Walter Scott's guests "burned the water" by Abbotsford at night, one man in the boat held a burning torch over the river. The inquiring salmon would shoot up his head out of the stream; and promptly speared. And I have been told that salmon will rise to a bit of scarlet cloth as readily as to the most artistic fly. In either case, it seems difficult to find a rational explanation. No salmon ever made a hearty meal of a torch or of scarlet cloth, or of anything remotely resembling these objects. We know very little of the mysteries of the animal consciousness, but on the face of it, it would seem that the fish rises to the torch and to the bit of scarlet out of idle curiosity. He certainly cannot mistake either for his mate.

Many of us have resigned ourselves to the fact that the great fame of Lord Verulam must suffer some diminution. We had brought ourselves, reluctantly, to acknowledge that the claim that Bacon wrote Shakespeare, the Authorised Version of the Bible, Montaigne's *Essays*, Cervantes' *Don Quixote*; in fact all the literature of the age, native and foreign, could not be substantiated. But it seems a little hard that his tercentenary should be celebrated by the total denial of his scientific eminence. Here, at least, Bacon seemed secure; but now we are told that he was, scientifically, a native of the dark ages. He thought that the skin of the wolf would cure stomach-ache—because wolves have good digestions. He laughed at Copernicus, Kepler, Galileo and Harvey; at all the true science of his time. Alas! poor Bacon.

Yet he uttered one sentence of the profoundest wisdom, one of the wisest sayings that has ever been spoken. He said that true beauty could not exist without the element of strangeness; and in that phrase he gives us the key to all life and all art.

There is some difficulty, I understand, about the new-old name of the town where we land in Ireland, if we have travelled via Holyhead. We used to call it Kingstown, we are now told that its name is Dun Leaoghaire. Why not solve the problem by continuing to spell it Kingstown and pronouncing it Dun Leaoghaire—if we can?

Seven

May 2, 1926

Writing in *The Observer* of last week, Mr. A. H. Fox-Strangways acknowledges that musicians are guilty of using technical terms. Somebody, it seems, has been asking him why he doesn't say what he means; instead of saying "arpeggio"; which signifies, I suppose, "harp-fashion." But every art, every craft has its technical vocabulary. The parson keeps a terrier which has nothing to do with dogs, since it is an account of the possessions (terrae) of his parish. Some years ago, logicians were highly interested in discussing the "thorough-going quantification of the predicate"; and architects, as Mr. Fox-Strangways points out, will talk of soffits, crockets, and corbels. Indeed, I have known them in their cups, to babble of pargetting.

The word of art is not to be avoided. Billingsgate has long been renowned for a certain curious choice of words: Thus Pope in "The Dunciad":—

There stirpt Fair rhetoric languish'd on the ground:
Her blunted arms by sophistry are borne,
And shameless Billingsgate her robes adorn.

But I do not refer to the fabled eloquence of the Market. I was looking through the list of prices the other day, and amongst friendly and familiar salmon, soles, turbot, and mullet I was shocked to encounter Witches and Megrims. They are cheap, quotations running from three to six shillings a stone; but at any price they would surely be a dreadful bargain; if they were really what they seem.

A strange thing once happened to me at Billingsgate. I had to see one of the Dutchmen who, by a mysterious and customary right, anchor their eel-boats just off Billingsgates Wharf. The boats were out in the river, and I asked a man on the landing stage how I was to attract their attention. "Just call out 'Dutchman, ahoy!'" said he. I did so, and it worked all right and seemed to give no offense—but I never thought such words would fall from my lips. "Ahoy!" "avast" "swabs" "lubbers" "Davy Jones's locker"; I had thought all this the language of transpontine melodrama, not of life. Besides, there seems something very coarse in addressing a Dutchman as "Dutchman."

...

When Smike and Nicholas Nickleby went on the stage they received between them the sum of a pound a week; this salary including payment for Nicholas's work as a theatre playwright. Things had improved a little, though not very much, in the early days of Sir Squire Bancroft. The Crummels company flourished, I take it, in the 'twenties of the last century; it was early in the 'sixties that the young Bancroft was paid eleven shillings a week. He and two friends, earning between them thirty-three shillings a week, lived together, and Sir Squire used to tell how he catered for the household, once buying a hake for fourpence, a chicken for sevenpence.

Twenty-five years ago strollers were still able to live economically. In 1901 I was one of a party of four who shared dim but comfortable rooms in an old house in Ipswich. We had enough to eat, and though our supper sausage was mysterious, it was savoury. At the end of the week, the bill was produced and divided up. Our board and lodging had cost each of us exactly eleven shillings.

Words, like books, have their peculiar fates. "Who would fardels bear?" asks Hamlet, and the only other place in which I have encountered the word is in the middle eighteenth century trial of Elizabeth Canning for perjury. A Dorsetshire witness described the old gypsy, Mary Squires, as carrying "a little fardle." And then there are words that survive only in a restricted and singular way. We never talk now of any thing being "replete" with anything; but a very few years ago I saw a notice board outside a big block of flats, proclaiming them to be "replete with every modern luxury and convenience." And I am delighted to see that Messers. Christie still sell by auction "objects of vertu," by which they mean watches, miniatures, snuff-boxes. Pictures are not objects of vertu, nor is gold or silver plate, nor is a diamond necklace. But an eighteenth-century paste necklace, I suppose, would certainly be such an object.

"Vertu" reminds me of an interesting, though snuffling, paragraph in Trench, "The Study of Words." The Italians, says Trench—writing in 1851—call an artist a virtuoso, a virtuous man, a picture gallery or museum guide a cicerone, a Cicero. From these circumstances the future Archbishop deduces the corruption of the Italian people. He might have made his case stronger still by instancing the Italian word for a hired assassin, "bravo," a brave or fine man.

Interesting enough, but as I think, fallacious and on the verge of cant. Are we to infer that Messrs Christie and their clients are a corrupt generation because they call a snuff-box "an object of vertu"?

...

A very queer object has just been added to the oddities of London. The M. C. C. have built a new stand on the north of Lord's and they have just crowned it with a weathercock. This represents Time, bearing the scythe of convention, as breaking a wicket. The batsman is not visible, but the ball is clearly seen, and it is lying on the ground. But the wicket-keeper, breaking a wicket, must have the ball in his hand. Evidently, therefore, the man is Not Out, and panting Time toils after him in vain.

Eight

May 23, 1926

There are common terms, in everyday use, which seem to me to conceal the profoundest mysteries. For example, "instinct." What is instinct?

The fact is I have been reading a very remarkable article on birds' nests, which has appeared recently. The writer tells how he found a last year's nest of the long-tailed tit and thoroughly examined it. The whole nest weighed an ounce. The main fabric was a firm but elastic felt, made of fine moss and spider cocoons. The exterior decoration consisted of bits of lichen; the interior was lined with 1,114 feathers, and also with rabbit fur, grass, oak leaves, and gorse pods. The staple of a skylark's nest, on the other hand, consisted of 1,610 pieces of grass.

Now the recipes of these two nests do not vary. The long-tailed tit never tries the skylark's way, and the skylark makes no use of spider silk. And the puzzle is how these miracles—so they seem to me—are accomplished. The bird, be it noted, has never seen a nest made; it has not learned how to make a nest. And consider the extreme complexity of the processes. The suckling of the young is a simple action, with a physical craving and a physical satisfaction urging the mother and the young at once. There is, perhaps, not much difficulty here; the word instinct might pass as an explanation, as a convenient piece of shorthand. But what is the faculty which directs this curious and laborious gathering together of so various a collection of odds and ends of the fields and hedgerows? What is there in the soul of the long-tailed tit which prescribes to it moss, spider silk, and feathers as its main raw materials, which bids the skylark rely on bits of grass? We are confronted by the problem of a consciousness which, to us, is utterly unfathomable.

"All my eye and Betty Marlin" is being discussed again. But I am glad to see that the old explanation, though still offered, is mentioned only with derision. This derivation was of the "God Encompasseth Us" (Goat and Compasses), "Chère Reine" (Charing Cross) school of philology. "All my eye and Betty Marlin," the story went, was a corrupt version of a pre-Reformation prayer to St. Martin. Sometimes the prayer began: "O mihi beate Martine" sometimes, "Ora mihi, beate Martine." There is no such prayer, nothing like such a prayer, in the old service books. The collect for Martinmas runs as follows: "O God, who seeest that of ourselves we are not able to help ourselves: mercifully grant that through the prayers of Saint Martin, Thy Confessor and Bishop, we may be defended against all adversity." The prayer, it will be noted, is not addressed to the saint; therefore the vocative "Beate" does not occur in it.

The truth probably is that "All my eye and Betty Marlin" was an eighteenth century catch word or cry, possibly a street song. It is idle to attempt any further explanation. Why "Betty Marlin"? Why "Whoa! Emma"? Why "What hot She bumps"?

An article in *The Observer* stated that the water-diviner or dowser is reaching something like an official status. In the Government of Bombay he is actually a highly-paid civil servant, and in England, it appears he is regularly employed by well-boring engineers and contractors. This, I think, is distinctly interesting. We used to be told that there was water to be found in most places if you dug deeply enough; hence, it was to be inferred, dowsing was all humbug.

But well-contractors and engineers must be supposed to know all that there is to know about the strange habits of water. They are hardly the kind of folk who would put humbugs on their pay-sheet.

An art critic, pouring over an illustrated Academy catalogue of fifty years ago, points out that the pictures which interested did so in virtue of their telling a story. I think it is much the same to-day. It certainly was so the day before yesterday. I found myself at Burlington House in one of the gloomiest of the later war periods. Everything seemed crashing about us; we were in the agonies of a new world that was being born of blood and iron and fire. But in the Academy all was peace. I saw pictures on the walls that were replicas rather than variants of pictures I admired in 1880. There were sandy lions crouching on sandy rocks, and there were boatmen on the Cornish coast.

I stopped in front of this latter picture; I have always liked it, from 1880 onwards. A beautiful sea—blue, green, olive, purple; rugged grey rocks; rugged figures in a dancing boat doing something with the oars. And as I gazed an old clergyman and his wife, evidently from the country, came up and joined me.

"What do they want to do with the boat?" said one.

"Get it out to sea, of course," answered the other.

"Well, I think they want to get to land."

"Nonsense!" said the old gentleman, rather tartly; and the two moved on.

They were trying to make a story out of a 'scape! I felt that England stood in the old ways, in spite of all the terrors and wild years; and I passed from the Academy a happier man than when I entered it.

Nine

May 30, 1926

It is interesting to find in the recently published "History of English Wallpaper" that this device for beautifying a bare wall goes back to the early years of the sixteenth century. There is nothing more to my taste than this mode of research into the minor things of life. I was talking the other day to a friend about that passage in "Cranford" which describes how that fine old yeoman, Mr. Holbrook, ate his peas with his knife, a knife made specially for the purpose, and with a large, round end. My friend remembered seeing such knives less than thirty years ago. They were not used, but remained in the drawer of the kitchen dresser: old-fashioned people did not like to throw away anything. The broad end had a marked curve to the right, and perhaps we should find the pea knife as difficult to use as Chinese chopsticks.

Of course, the forks of our forefathers were useless for pea-eating purposes; they had only two prongs. And a Templar tells me that even such forks as these were novelties in the Inner Temple Hall of fifty years ago. There were no forks before that. You held your meat down with a spoon, cut it up with a knife, and then ate it with the spoon.

But as to wallpaper: a terrible variety was recommended by Gray, the poet, to a friend. Gray had found some "stucco paper" at threepence a yard. It represented Gothic arches and niches, and Gray says that it is "rather pretty and nearly Gothic"—and, I should add, very funny. The early attempts at the revival of the Gothic spirit always entertain me. Why doesn't somebody write a history of Sham Gothic, amply illustrated? There would be plates of Abbotsford, where the massive oak beams in the interior were really made of plaster of Paris, and certainly plates of Walpole's Strawberry Hill villa, one of the earliest performances of this queer architecture. There is a very fine example in Staple Inn—a doorway with rich mouldings, which would make a Gothic cat laugh. And look at the original frontispiece to "Pickwick." The picture is framed in an arch very much of the Staple Inn pattern; and the glazed bookcase behind Mr. Pickwick and Sam Weller shows strong traces of the Gothic idea. And then there is Wemmick's house at Walworth. I do not know that this has ever been delineated by an artist; it was a Gothic castle, even what the French call a *château fort*; for Wemmick contemplated "the little place" being besieged.

A literary critic expresses a wish that authors would give the scenes of their stories their real names; that is, that if you are writing a tale about Stow-on-the-Wold, you should call it Stow-on-the-Wold; not Chipping Wolden. The critic—a lady, I take it—has been reading "The Reluctant Imposter," by Muriel Hine, and speaks of the pleasure she found in reading of a Provençal town where she once spent a delightful holiday, of the very hat-shop in a South Coast watering-place, where the writer bought hats; of the curiosity shops in the back lanes where she collected antiques.

And there seems something in this point of view. Zola, I believe, wished that he had called Aix in Provence Aix, instead of inventing the name Plassans. And yet many authors have given themselves infinite trouble in coining names for the actual places they describe. Look at the map, "The Wessex of the Novels," appended to Hardy's works. It contains three or four dozen invented place-names, ranging from Exonberry in the south to Christminster in the north—otherwise, from Exeter to Oxford; from Downstaple in the west to Wintoncester in the east—or from Barnstable to Winchester.

And there are doubtless reasons for following this course. There is the fear that if your towns are to be discovered on the map then people will conclude that your characters are to be discovered in the towns. If you talk of the Dean of Winchester, then people will note other data in the tale, point out the particular dean you had in your mind; and possibly the venerable man may issue from the retirement of a country living and cause you to be heavily cast in damages and costs. But I do not think this consideration entered into the mind of Thomas Hardy: the map I have mentioned, very names themselves in many cases make the secret no secret at all. And Hardy's characters—as I conjecture—are not portraits of actual men. The fact is, I believe, that the severest struggles of the great writer are concerned with getting away from actuality in order to attain reality. Dorchester is the actual town; Casterbridge the real town.

Ten

June 6, 1926

Mr. A. E. Evans, speaking at the Association of Teachers in Technical Institutions, says that wireless operators, seamen, and rescuers in mines are as good as Homer, Virgil, and Horace. I think he states the position over modestly. I have said before, and I am not ashamed to say again, fur coats are never so much warmer than Sapphics, Alcaics, or Ionics *a minore*. And all businessmen know too well that Herodotus won't wash clothes.

"Ignoramus," writing in last Sunday's *Observer*, sets me some hard puzzles. He wants to know the origin of "Sophy-Slap-Cabbage," "Nosey Parker," and "Kelly, K-E-L-L-Y." Well, "Kelly" comes from a music hall song, "Has anybody here seen Kelly?" The choice of the name, Kelly, must be assigned to the taste and fancy of the unknown author. There are things without reason in the universe: it would be idle to inquire why they sang nearly fifty years ago of the two Obadiahs, rather than the two Hezekiahs, or of the two Zephaniahs. "Nosey Parker," an inquisitive person: "nosey" is clear enough, but I can offer no solution of "Parker." It is true that formerly the stage servant was often called Parker, and servants are supposed to be inquisitive as to their masters' affairs; but I offer this solution doubtfully. "Sophy-Slap-Cabbage" is strange to me; I know her as "Mother Slap-Cabbage." The image suggested is of a fat, slovenly, down-at-heel old woman, busy over a greasy sink in an area back kitchen. Once in a dressing room I heard the Second Fury—in the "Eumenides" of Æschylus—address the First Fury with the words: "Come along, Mother Slap-Cabbage." I am glad to note that the Second Fury has seen the error of his Pagan ways, and is now the Prior of Aosta in "St. Bernard."

In the same issue of *The Observer* a graver correspondent, Dr. Fournier D'Albe, notes that the cruder form of the Darwinian sexual selection theory is no longer held; when the male hummingbird gyrates he is not trying to attract the female, but simply catching flies. I remember once looking at the gorgeous gold and green and copper of the Autumn beach woods, and wondering who or what was to be attracted by these glowing colours—on this hypothesis, that the splendors of nature are purely utilitarian. And hence I was led to wonder whether the strange mingled fires of the opal, the green of the emerald, and the shimmering beauty of the pearl are designed by Nature to attract the wives of very wealthy men.

Sir Jagadis Bhose, an Indian poet and man of science, says that plants feel, that they have a nervous system, more acute than that of an oyster, less acute than the sensibility of a human being. It is a singular thought: Perhaps the cedar does sigh in Lebanon in fact, and not alone in the poet's fancy. But when Sir Jagadis—he sounds almost Morte-darthurian—declares that he can justify scientifically "the ancient dreamer," who said, "never beat a woman even with a flower, for who knows, which of the two suffers most," he is, surely, trifling. What on earth is the good of beating a woman with a flower? But, perhaps, the ancient dreamer had hollyhocks or sunflowers in mind. Well-grown specimens have stout stems that might be serviceable in mild cases.

The Archbishop of Canterbury has been saying very kind things about the stage and the people on the stage; and I think it is high time that the virtues of the actor should have the blessing of the Church. A long time ago, the tour was nearing its end; there was only, I think, a week to go, and then, for many of us, the Great Perhaps. At the matinee, just before the curtain went up, I observed an elder member of the company dancing a little dance in the wings, his countenance beaming with good humour and high spirits.

"You've had some good news, Mr. Lenville?" I remarked.

"No, old chap. Been around the agents all the morning: Nothing doing."

And he went on dancing gaily.

What does the Book say? "Take no thought for the morrow, for the morrow shall take thought for the things of itself."

It has often struck me that, in this matter of the stage, we are somewhat hard on the seventeenth century Puritans. It is true that they suppressed the drama, but they did so because they thought it amused people, and they held that all amusement was wicked. But at the same period in France all actors were ex-communicate, deprived of the Sacraments of the Church. And in our own age, Cardinal Manning defined play-acting as the defiling of a body that has been purified by Baptism.

Eleven

June 13, 1926

Why did Surrey schoolboys once conceal the spray of oak, the badge of the restored Charles II., on Oak Apple Day, till they were challenged to "show their shik-shak"? That is the problem proposed for my solution in last week's *Observer* by Mr. F. T. Corrie; and I confess at once, it defeats me. Mr. Corrie's suggestion that the concealment and disclosure constitute a ritual, originating in the period between King Charles's escape and restoration, is an extremely ingenious one. By this method, it is suggested, one Royalist was enabled to know another in the dangerous days of Cromwell.

It might be so. It is conjectured that in the second century of our era, in the Roman tavern two strangers might be seated at a table. One might dip his finger into the winecup, and absent-mindedly draw the outline of a Fish upon the board. The other might glance at his neighbour and take no further note of him and his doings. Or, he might on his side, dabble his finger in his wine, and draw the five letters that spell fish in Greek: and then the two Christians would recognize one another. So, according to the late Professor Browne, the persecuted Babis of Persia used to draw diagrams on the sand; figures which meant nothing to an outsider, everything to a fellow Babi.

Then as to the term "shik-shak": here is a puzzle within a puzzle. At Cheltingham, seventy or eighty years ago, Oak Apple Day was called Shik-Shak Day. There is something odd and Babylonish about the sound and shape of the word. I hesitate—and no more than hesitate—conjecture that both the word "shik-shak" and the wearing of the oak are of high antiquity, appropriated in the seventeenth century to King Charles II., as the ancient observance of the bonfire was appropriated in the same century to Guy Fawkes. And, by the way, there is—or was—a theory that the Master's Degree in Freemasonry was founded on the death of the first Charles and the Restoration of the second; for this there is clearly nothing to be said.

"Teeftallow," a new book with an odd name, deals with Tennessee, that strange State where they sing old English songs and dance old English dances that have not been sung or seen in old England for a hundred years or more. Tennessee must be full of queer things. Why do they talk there of "we un" and "you uns"? Presumably, the idiom is of English origin; but I have never heard of its use in England, either in the present or the past.

And then, again, there is the odd Tennessee etiquette of smoking for ladies. The old mountain farmer was regretting his daughter's flighty ways. "She wants to smoke cigarettes," he said, "but I tell her I won't stand for that: a corn cob pipe was good enough for her mother, and it has got to be good enough for her." And legal procedure has its difficulties in the State. An American friend of mine owns land in Tennessee.

"Well," he said to me reflectively, "I shall have to foreclose on Old Buck Dunlap this fall. He hasn't paid me a cent for years, and if I don't foreclose, the land will go to him. But I'm not going to be around. Old Buck has got nine notches on his gun already. I don't want to be the tenth."

Mr. H. A. L. Fisher is evidently of the True Church of Literature; but I think he is a little bit of an ultramontane. He is reported to have said that it was not necessary for his enjoyment that literature should have sense, provided it had music. On the face of it, this seems to me that fine literature may be nonsense, provided that it be sonorous nonsense. Well, Pater declares that in the last resort all the arts are to be referred to music; and yet we see that all the arts save music must have "sense," or its analogical equivalent. Your picture of a tree, for example, must be recognisably a tree, though there must be much more in it than the likeness of trunk, limbs, boughs, twigs, leaves; the something more being the thrill of emotion which the artist experienced in contemplating the tree, and this something more being the essence of the picture, that which imparts to it all its merit. Curiously, the only strict analogy to music in another art is a decorative pattern, as, for example, in a Persian carpet, or the interlaced ornament of the Celts. In neither of these is there "sense," but then, perhaps, neither of these is an affair of art, but rather of craft.

Yet it is true that on the rarest and highest peaks of literature sense is almost dissolved—not into nonsense, but into a mysterious super-sense. In Coleridge's "Kubla Khan" and in Keats's magistral "Ode to a Nightingale," you have the quintessence of that which is finest in literature; but what are magic casements? Where are faery lands forlorn? Perhaps literature on the heights goes back, in a way, to the depths from which it rose; not to a plain tale of simple circumstances; but to an incantation chanted in the darkness, a song that spoke not to the intellect, but to the spirit of man.

Twelve

June 20, 1926

It is improbable, I suppose, that pills and plasters made of earth are of high therapeutic value. But the villagers of Quarto Disoccavo, near Naples, are swallowing the earth pills and plastering themselves with the earth ointment, and, like Mr. Pickwick after the Bath waters, declare that they are a great deal better.

This new treatment is the invention of a local priest, Don Luigi Garofalo. He says that man being dust, earth is good for him, more particularly this very special earth of Pozzuoli. And his patients (who pay nothing for the treatment) agree that the earth pills and ointments are good for paralysis and toothache and tuberculosis and a broken leg. As I suggest, they are probably wrong. It's hardly within the limits of possibility that the same dose should cure toothache and tuberculosis. And yet again these simple peasants are probably right. If you are quite sure that something—anything—will do you good, a cure will very often be affected. Sometimes it is necessary to swallow anything or to rub anything on the aching limb. What is the Coué formula? "Pain going," or "every day and in every way I am getting better and better." I am told that many people have benefited greatly by uttering these phrases in the manner prescribed; and I am quite ready to believe that this is so. I was most interested to see that so imminent a physician as Dr. Mary Scharlieb has recently declared that liver and stomach troubles are often the result, not of errors of diet, but of errors of thought. I feel quite sure that I bored myself into jaundice a good many years ago. You can think yourself into illness, you can think yourself into health. The little thieving guttersnipe in Drury-lane was dragged into the chemist's shop and given, in a vessel adorned with unknown symbols, a clear draught, which he was told he would remember till the day of his death. He almost died that very night, and the next morning his mother brought a policeman round to the chemist's shop. But the cabalistic vessel—a graduated glass—had merely contained Aqua Pura, and the earth pills of Don Luigi Garofalo are simply the chemist's treatment benevolently reversed.

The "Car and Country" correspondent of *The Observer* speaks a little roughly in his last week's article of some of the place names of my native land: Llanfihangeltorymynydd, Cwmcarvan, Caerwent. But what can be simpler than Llanfihangeltorymynydd: The Church of St. Michael the Archangel by the crag of the mountain? Surely, this is a more dignified address than Tooting. I admit that here and there in Gwent we have some place-names which the Saxon might term teasers. Some years ago, I was talking to the Polish Ambassador, and mentioned that well-known industrial town, Lodz. He looked puzzled for a moment and then remarked: "we call it Wooj." I was not going to be crowed over, even by an Ambassador. I wrote down on a piece of paper the word Mynyddysllwyn—and asked His Excellency what he made of it. He was dumb.

Another Celtic matter. Mr. John Walker, F. S. A., also writing in *The Observer*, is annoyed because Irishmen quietly assume, he declares, that the early Celtic Church was, necessarily, a purely Irish product. Well, I think St. Columba came from Ireland to Iona, and I believe that it is acknowledged that the term "Scoti" might be applied in those early ages to Scots and Irish indifferently. The language was, practically, one. The old Highland soldier, recalling his service in Ireland in '98, said it seemed a pity to have to shoot such a fine man, "and men that spoke a prettier Gaelic than what ye'll hear in many of the Isles"—that is the Hebrides. But the early Celtic Church extended not only over Scotland and Ireland, but through Wales and Brittany. It is one of the few mysteries left in the world. It was not the "Garrison Church" of the Roman occupation of Britain. That church sent three diocesan bishops to the Council of Arles in the fourth century; the Celtic Church of the fifth, sixth, and seventh centuries was non-diocesan. It had bishops, naturally and necessarily, but it was ruled by abbots, who are not always of the episcopal order, and its Liturgy must remain a matter of conjecture. The Anglo-Roman Church, arriving from St. Augustine's mission, appears to have made a clean sweep of the Celtic service-books. The last mention of the Rite dates from the twelfth century. There was then, says the chronicler, a church in Glasgow where the clergy used "nescioquo ritu barbaro"—outlandish service or other. He doesn't know what this service was like, and—it's quite clear—he doesn't care.

Some authors have tried to press "barbaro" too far. They will have it that the word implies that the Celtic Rite was in Gaelic, not in Latin; but this is highly improbable. It was, I conjecture, a near relation of the Mozarabic Liturgy of Spain, which is still used occasionally in certain churches.

...

Letchworth Garden City has just come of age. I have never seen it, but I have seen a Garden City near London—and I would not live in it on any account. It looks to me like a backcloth. It has, I remember, pergolas for rambler roses, but I cannot treat them seriously. I believe stage hands and property men rush on every night at sunset and "strike" those pergolas amid the imprecations of a foaming stage manager.

There are real Garden Cities in England. In these you walk up to the old inn yard and find it changes into a country lane. The long street is interrupted here and there by green boughs waving over garden walls. Behind the houses, deep gardens descend to the brook, and across the wooden bridge are the meadows and the woods. Indeed, there are some rich remnants of a Garden City in London itself. St. John's Wood has been scarred of late by terrible blocks of flats that look like model prisons or up-to-date barracks, but many of its leafy, bowery ways are left, and their little white houses half hidden behind the garden wall and the green leaf.

Thirteen

June 27, 1926

The Turkish Board of Education, who are prescribing the school books of the Republic, must be incurable optimists. They declare that all historical works must be free from falsehoods. Such books are, probably, unprocurable. It is impossible to write history that is free from falsehood, when history departs from the mere skeleton of names and dates. We know, for example when George IV. was born, and when he died, but there is every reason to suppose that the Leigh Hunt, "fat Adonis of fifty" portrait of him is a falsehood. I think Walter Scott was the first person of the baronets created by him; he pensioned Coleridge; he honored literature. General Higginson remembers being patted on the head by King George, and he testifies that the monarch's face, though podgy, was essentially kind.

Then there is another historical falsehood on a bigger scale. It is almost accepted now that the Victorian age was an essentially prim and old-maidish period. It was nothing of the kind; either in life or in letters. The mid-Victorian came out of the theatre soon before midnight. He had a dozen or so of oysters and a pint of stout somewhere in the Haymarket, and then strolled on to Evan's in Convent Garden and ate and drank and smoked there till any hour of the morning. And the best work of Swinburne and Rossetti was mid-Victorian. It was not old-maidish; whatever else it may have been. But the people who talk of the primness of the mid-Victorians have probably never heard of Robert Buchanan or of his attack on the "Fleshly School."

The Turkish educational authorities have another stipulation to make as to the history text-books. They are to be free from falsehoods; furthermore, they are to contain no allegories. That means, I suppose, that young Turks are not to be taught anything in the manner of the allegory of the Belly and the Members— see "Coriolanus." But it is quite true that in literature allegory is a bad thing. Many people have thought that the merit of the "Pilgrim's Progress" is in its pious and edifying moral. This is a mistake. We enjoy Bunyan's masterpiece in spite of the allegory, in spite of such names as Mr. Facing-both-ways. We enjoy it as a masterpiece of the picaresque, told in the most vivid English; and we enjoy it because of the happy ending, a thing that every good man loves in a book. Cervantes should have left Don Quixote alive; still dreaming his wonderful dream.

Dr. Armitage Robinson, the Dean of Wells, is no doubt right in concluding, in his "Glastonbury Legends," that the St. Joseph of Arimathea connection and the Arthurian connection were comparatively late. I do not think that we can trace the legend linking St. Joseph with Glastonbury beyond William of Malmesbury, who wrote about 1130. And as to King Arthur, I believe that we owe his connection with Glastonbury to a singular confusion. There can be no doubt that Arthur was a mystic figure to the Celts, long before the Anglo-Norman romancers interested themselves in Welsh folklore. The early Welsh poem, "Y Beddau" (The Graves) describes the place of sepulture of many heroes, including, if I remember, that of Beddwyr, or Bedivere, but it warns us: "vain is it to seek for the grave of Arthur." King Arthur, then, was translated, taken to Paradise, or Avalon. But the Celtic name of Glastonbury was Avalon, in its literal mundane sense of "apple-orchard"—there is a town of the same name in Burgundy—and hence the legend which makes Glastonbury the burial place of King Arthur.

But the one thing to be aware of in considering the Arthurian Legend or the Grail Legend, is the interpretation of the "Pagan" school. No doubt there are pre-Christian elements in both myths. No doubt ἰδιώταις meant in Greece a man who held no public office. But this fact throws no light on our "idiot"; and the pagan origins of the Grail legend throw no light on the twelfth and thirteenth century romances one may, ultimately, derive from the other; but the sense has changed.

But life is full of problems. There is the Grail complex, of which we have been speaking—and the other day, as I paced along a quiet, leafy and a decorous byway behind Lord's, I noted with amazement that the road was strewn with women's battered and disreputable hats. Not in a cluster, but discreet, with an interval of a hundred yards or more between shabby straw and villainous velveteen. Had there been a running flight or some such pretty, irregular kind of warfare; alcoholic amazons being the warriors? Probably, we will never know.

Yet another problem: "a poor thing, not my own." How many people can correct this misquotation; offhand, and without book? And again: have we in this and in "to-morrow to fresh fields and pastures new" instances of what may be called folk-misquotation, or can we trace each to the error of an individual?

...

Lady Forster, wife of the former Governor-General of Australia, says that good cooking does not mean rich cooking. Here is a truth which is far from being generally known. Many of us are under the impression that a really fine dinner must consist of a number of elaborate messes; and also that French cookery is distinguished by its rich complexity. These are errors. The average, comfortably-off French household sits down at lunch to bread and butter, sardine, and three or four radishes. Then follows an omelet exquisitely made, and the fish, often not exquisite in itself, is attractive because the frying of it is perfect. A mutton cutlet and fried potatoes is often the next dish; and this may be followed by green peas or by velvety, delicious spinach. After the spinach, there may be cold chicken before the cheese and the pears. An admirable meal, but neither "messy" nor elaborate.

Fourteen

July 4, 1926

Its may be remembered that David Copperfield, while at Dr. Strong's school, once took tea with Uriah Heep and his mother. "Phiz," the artist, shows us the scene at the moment when Mr. Micawber, bland and beaming, looks in at the open door. The Heeps, of course, were at that period of the story, quite poor people. The furniture of the room is very simple. There is the tea-table, a bureau above it, and five plain-looking chairs. To young David the room had a "bare, pinched, spare look."

It was to emphasise the poverty-stricken aspect of the place that the artist drew the chairs of that particular pattern. For those chairs were about 120 years old, and only poor people, who could afford nothing better, would give house-room to such shabby furniture. And—here is the queer thing—the other day Messrs. Hampton sold eight of these chairs for one thousand and sixty guineas. For Uriah's room, "half parlour, half kitchen," was furnished with chairs that were undoubted Queen Anne. Fifty years ago, I remember some people grumbling because they could not afford to buy decent new furniture. Their chairs and tables were pure Sheraton.

Mister J. H. Roberts, of Newport, a kindly fellow-countryman of mine, has set me right as to the translation of one of our simple Monmouthshire's place-names, Llanfihangeltorymynydd. This, says Mr. Roberts, does not mean, "the church of St. Michael the Archangel on the crag of the mountain," but "the Church of St. Michael the Archangel in the gap of the mountain"; and so I put the matter on record, lest any go astray as to Llanfihangeltorymynydd. And Mr. Roberts adds that to the older generation of Welsh country folk such a gap in the mountains was known as "Y Gymwynas"—the Favour. "To the old peasants, the Mighty Sculptor of the rocks had purposely cloven the mountain in twain, as a Favour to them, enabling them to walk from vale to vale, avoiding a weary climb over the towering cliffs."

Last week, as I read, a conference was held on the proposal to establish a school of African languages in London. I do not envy the students of the proposed school. The Black Grammar is a highly complicated work. Take the pronoun "I" for example. We are content with plain "I" in all the emergencies of speech, save when, in moments of forgetfulness, we say "me." But in Ngamba-Ngamba things are very different. Thus—or somewhat thus:—

> Nga = I.
> Noliu = I, your fellow villager.
> Mbo = I, a stranger.
> Cha = I, a young man.
> Nki = I, an elderly man.
> Ibambo = I, an infant under five.

And, to return for a moment to our former topic; I was once discussing with an arrant Saxon the curious mutation of consonants in the Welsh tongue. He said grimly: "the syntax of savages is always complicated."

The "Jubilee of the Restoration of the Church of St. Etheldreda, Ely-place, Holborn, to the Roman Catholic faith," has just been celebrated. If I remember rightly, the Royal Arms, formerly displayed in the church in its Anglican days, now stand in the porch, with an inscription to the effect that this symbol of the royal headship in matters ecclesiastical has no longer any right within the sacred place. But Royal Arms in a church have not necessarily this significance. I have seen a reproduction of an old print of Lyons Cathedral, dating from 1720 or thereabouts. The high altar, devoid of cross, candles, other ornaments, stands on the chord of the apse. Behind it, against the wall, are the seats of the clergy; and in the center, the archbishop's throne. And the decoration at the back of the throne consists of three lilies, the Royal Arms of France. Indeed, it was common enough in the Middle Ages for Mass vestments to be richly embroidered with the armorial bearings of the donor; I've seen chasubles and dalmatics or, with leopards gules—and ramping.

Our Tractarians erred in much the same way as the authorities of St. Etheldreda's when they (most unhappily) began to set their churches in order. They thought beadles were Protestant, so they swept them away. They should have gone to France and seen the splendid Suisse, who is nothing more or less than a beadle. It was a Tractarian vicar who banished the old players of violins and serpents from the gallery of the Parish Church in "Under the Greenwood Tree." Mr. Maybold, no doubt, thought the Serpent was a Protestant Serpent; but if he had investigated the matter he would have found that this instrument was esteemed in France as an invaluable support to the Plain Chant, and that a "Méthode du Serpent" had been published at Paris in the eighteenth century.

I quote the following from an article called "Help for the Camper," published lately:—

Ropes shrink when wet, so if it is raining when you go to bed loosen the guy lines and knock in the pegs. ... If it continues to rain during the night take another look around about 3 a.m. It sounds cold and miserable, but not nearly so cold or miserable as having your tent blown in on you when you are not expecting it.

And this is supposed to be a form of pleasure: this taking of immense pains in order to be exquisitely uncomfortable. I often wonder what would be said if criminals at the Old Bailey were sentenced, not to gaol, but to a course of sports and pastimes. Supposing the judge said: "John Smith, I can only regard you as a monster of cruelty, on whom leniency would be wasted. The sentence upon you is that you go into camp for the remainder of the summer. You may say that the cold, wet, and exposure are likely to be fatal to a man of your constitution. I agree that such is the case; but you should have thought of that before you endeavoured to burn your unfortunate wife alive."

But the truth is that voluntary discomfort, misery, danger, make the choicest delights of most Englishmen.

A good many years ago, there was a foot race between, I think, Windsor and Shepherd's Bush. The distance between the two places is 26 miles. By one road—there is a shortcut—distance between Marathon and Athens is 26 miles. So, perhaps, there was some justification for giving the name of Marathon to the Windsor—Shepherd's Bush event. But I am very sure that there is no justification whatever for calling a four-in-hand competition the "Coaching Marathon." The coaches were driven from Richmond Hill to Olympia. The latter name suggests the glory that was Greece, but the distance between the two points is six miles, not twenty-six. Moreover, there was no question of speed in the contest, which was judged on the make, shape, and condition of the horses and the smartness of the coaches and harness. However, I suppose we are within reasonable distance of the Shoveha'penny Marathon.

Fifteen

July 11, 1926

An odd advertisement appeared a few days ago in the "Personal" or "Agony" column of a daily paper. It was thus:—

ASHLAR (PERFECT). Poor and distressed. Will CHILDREN of WIDOW subscribe. Remit to XY, etc.

Now, at first sight, there seems something a little obscure in the diction of this appeal. But it is really quite simple. Ashlar, or (as the Middle Ages spelt it), achiler, is a word for stone. There are two kinds of ashlar, the rough ashlar, the stone as it comes out of the quarry, and the smooth, or perfect, ashlar that has been shaped and justified by the craftsman's tools. Cf. (as the school books say) the famous dictum of Robertus de Fluctibus, or Robert Flood, who flourished in the early part of the seventeenth century, and was thought to have had a good deal to do with the Rosicrucians: *Transmutemini, transmutemini de lapidibus mortuis in lapides phliosophicos vivos:* Be ye changed, be ye changed from dead stones into living and life-giving stones. Compare also the verse of the famous hymn, *Cœlestis Urbs Hierusalem*, beginning, *Scalpri salubris ictibus:*—

> Many a blow and biting sculpture
> Polished well these stones elect,
> Ere in place they were compacted
> By their heavenly architect

That, I hope, makes "Ashlar" quite clear. As for the Widow: To the best of my belief nobody even knows her name. But she left an enormous family of children, all boys, who survive her.

It was melancholy to read in last week's *Observer* of the "improvements" performed and contemplated at East Sheen Common. Here is a wonderful wild place, full of wild plants and wild life, close to London, and most unwisely, the Urban District Council of Barnes has been given powers to make the common "more pleasant." One needs no Socrates to elicit an urban council's definition of "more pleasant." To quote the correspondent of *The Observer*: "one delightful rude path with bushes at the side has been converted into a straight broad (but

scarcely used) road; and stiff chestnuts—now looking very unhealthy—
have been planted along the sides." And gorse and heather have been
grubbed up, and the thick hedgerows, where the sweet birds still sing,
are threatened. I know quite well what affect the Urban Council has
in its mind. It is realized in perfection on Clapham Common, the day
after the August Bank Holiday. Railings all about, a bare expanse of
sorry turf stamped into scabby patches, and exactly one million pieces
of torn paper.

Good people, I believe, have wondered who it is to take the part of
the Barbarians in destroying and renewing our civilization. The Huns,
the Vandals, and the Goths pulled the Roman order down into ruin;
but where now shall we find peoples who will do the work of Vandals,
Huns, and Goths? Clearly, we shall be reformed from within; Urban
District Councils. The Complete Barbarian will not be lacking.

The work of devastation is going on everywhere. A Lavenham man
was telling me the other day of the ruin that is being worked in this
little, but noble, town. Lavenham is of the fifteenth century. It was rich
in that age, and money then expressed itself in beauty. And, even now,
they are tearing down one of the finest of the old Lavenham houses. It
is to be rebuilt in Enfield or Elstree, or Ealing: and the odd thing is that
the purchaser has sense enough to admire the beauty of the old house,
and not sense enough to see that this beauty will cease to exist in the
raw surroundings of a modern suburb. A Gothic statue from the west
front of a cathedral placed among the fashion dummies of a Regent-
street shop front would be a painful and distressing spectacle.

A bottle of wine, said to be at least 200 years old, has been discovered
under a house in Gresham-street—once Cateaton-steet, where the
great house of Bilson and Slum, Tom Smart's employers, carried on
their business. The bottle, it is said, retained a dark fluid, which smelt
decidedly of port. I have met a far older wine. A well-known firm of
wine merchants have in their possession a few bottles of Steinwein,
purchased, I think, during a seller clearance of the royal house of
Saxony. And this wine was of the famous vintage of 1545. I did not
taste it, but I was assured that it was still wine, though its original riches
had turned to poverty. Then there is a West End firm which treasures a
bottle of claret dug up on the field of Philliphaugh, of a vintage about
a hundred years later than the Steinwein. I do not know whether the
condition of the wine has been tested.

The ancient Italians clearly understood the affair of the vine better than their descendants. At Trimalchios' Banquet there was a wine labeled: *Opimianum Falernum Annos Centum*. The Falernum of the Italian restaurant is not famous even now, but I feel sure that it would not be better by a hundred years keeping.

A curious problem is suggested by the ninth century document lately discovered in Italy and quoted in *The Observer* of last Sunday. Professor Gallo, discoverer, hails the document as almost the "birth certificate of the Italian language," by which he means, I suppose, the first written example which shows traces of modern Italian, no doubt, a far worse jargon had long been in colloquial use. Still, the discovery is queer enough and its idiom: "Potestate me abea de prendere"; this means, no doubt, "had power to take me."

And now for the problem. The Apostle strictly enjoins that the service of the Christian Church shall be in a language understood by the congregation. "Else when thou shalt bless with the spirit, how shall he that occupieth the room of the unlearned say Amen at the giving of thanks, seeing he understandeth not what thou sayest?" [1] There is no doubt as to the meaning here; there is also no doubt that the Latin Rite makes use of a language which has been unintelligible to the unlearned for many hundreds of years. Indeed, there is another Rite the intelligibility of which is beginning to be questioned; it is sad that there are many who do not understand what "prevent us, O Lord, all our doings," and "thereto I plight thee my troth" mean. [2]

Still; what were the churchmen of the seventh, eighth, and ninth centuries to do? They could not translate the Missal and the Breviary into this "abea de prendere" jargon; they would have esteemed a service in such an ugly patois as horribly irreverent. And, if we come to think of it, an Englishman stationed in China would be somewhat perturbed if he heard the priest sing:

Topside hearts

And the choir responded:—

Topside Joss hab got.

So the problem of those early ecclesiastics remain unsolved.

---

1 1 Corinthians 14:16 (King James Version)
2 "Prevent us, O Lord" is a prayer from the 1662 Book of Common Prayer. "Prevent" is from the Latin "pre-venire or "go before." "Thereto I plight thee my troth," forms part of the wedding vows in the Anglican Church and signifies the promise to marry one another in faithfulness.

Sixteen

July 18, 1926

Jeering Jack Jones replied to the proclamation of the Royal Assent to the Eight Hours Bill—Le Roy le veult—with the wholly irreverent response: "Honi soit que mal y pense," and I believe that some of those present were inclined to smile at Jack's pronunciation of the Norman French motto. But the question of the right manner of uttering this antique dialect is a difficult one. I have often been at the Old Bailey— let me say at once that I was never cast for what actors would call "the heavy lead"—and have heard with sorrow the appointed functionary proclaiming, "O yea, O yea, O yea." This is all wrong: he should say, "O yes, O yes, O yes." The final letter was pronounced. So we have tennis from "tenez," the cry of the player in the service court: "Take it" or, as we should say, "Play!"

And why is the motto of the Order of the Garter always mistranslated? It does not mean: Evil be to him who evil thinks. It means: Shamed be he that thinks ill of it.

But this motto and the Parliamentary formula are in good, though archaic, French. This is more than can be said of the extraordinary jargon of the old Law Reports. It is sometimes called Law Latin, sometimes Law French; I do not think Yiddish, Early Latin-Italian, or Pigeon English can compare with its rich absurdity. I remember a choice example in one of the notes to Pepys. At an Assizes Court (c. 1630) the prisoner "ject un brickbat fuit immediatement drawn par Noy, Attorney General." I believe the misguided prisoner came to a bad end. His "dexter manus" was "ampute," and he was "hange sur un gibbet."

Somebody has been writing to the paper to the effect that the legends about Dick Whittington are mythical. The critic points out that the tale of the friendly cat was not mentioned (in print) before 1604; while Whittington died in 1423. And, no doubt, the cat is wholly mythical; but I should suspect that the tale dates far back beyond the fifteenth century. The notion of a friendly alliance between man and beast must be of vast antiquity; it belongs to the period when all the fairy tales began: Puss-in-Boots helped the Marquis of Carabas as the cat helped Whittington. The puzzle is, how an age-old legend became appropriated to solid Richard Whittington, Mercer, four times mayor, benefactor of St. Bartholomew's Hospital, founder of the College of St. Spirit and St. Mary, of an almshouse called God's Hospital, builder of a noble library for the house of the Greyfriars, beautifier by will of the Guildhall, and author of many other benefits to Londoners.

Professor Ola Opsjon, a Norwegian authority on Runic inscriptions, says that the Norseman not only discovered America long before Columbus but that some of them crossed from sea to sea, and left a monument with their simple story inscribed in "indelible paint" near Spokane, in the state of Washington. It may be so; but *Timeo Danaos et Runa ferentes*. "Danaos," of course, is to be rendered "the Danes, or Norwegians," as in the celebrated schoolboy translation.

There are all sorts of queer things—very queer things—in Mr. M. Oldfield Howey's "The Encircled Serpent." It is all about serpent symbolism and serpent worship in all lands and in all ages. But I do not think I should have quoted Madam Blavatsky as a serious authority, nor that other writer who says that the French word *enfer* means "one fire." However, I have noticed that an eccentric etymology "goes" with certain doctrines. I was once casting scorn on the theory that the English are the Lost Ten Tribes of Israel. It was pointed out to me that "Saxon" is obviously a contraction of "Isaacson." I had no more to say; or, at all events, did not say it. So with the Baconians. One of them, to whom I shall be ever grateful, has shown that "Don Quixote" is, in fact, "d'un qui s'ôte," about the man who keeps out of the way—Bacon, of course.

The actors who took apart in the "Œdipus at Colonus" at the Scala wore the Greek tragic masks. They were heroes of the hot weather, but I think they were mistaken. The Greek open-air theatre held from ten to twenty thousand people. Many of them must have been at a considerable distance from the stage; so that if the principles had gone on in something like the make-up of the modern actor, and spoken their lines as a good modern actor speaks Shakespeare, nothing would have been seen, nothing would have been heard by the majority of the audience. Hence the buskin or "elevator" raising the actor to more than mortal height, hence the huge masks fitted with megaphones. And, no doubt, dialogue was uttered in a measured and sonorous chant. But none of these devices is required or desirable in a modern theatre of ordinary size.

About twenty-five years ago they were doing a spectacular piece called "The Relief of the Legations" at the theatre of the old Earl's Court Exhibition— a huge place. There was not much dialogue, I caught a scrap of it, which was delivered like this. "And—if—I—fall—tell—my—mother—I—died—at—the—post—of—duty." The actor intoned the words; and it struck me that this must have been the method of the Greek drama. Of course, there could have been no emotional expression in this slow and measured chant, but vocal emotion was not demanded of the actor anymore than it is demanded of the Minor Canon intoning, "When the wicked man."

Seventeen

July 25, 1926

"Observator," writing in last week's *Observer* about the gentleman who was dug out of the ice of the Alps a hundred years ago and was restored to life after a frozen repose of 200 years, has many interesting parallels to offer: The Seven Sleepers, Peter Klaus, Rip Van Winkle, and others. A curious example of the legend is to be found in Walter Mapp's "De Nugis Curialium" (late twelfth century). Here the sleeper is a British king who passes a night in Fairyland. Coming forth in the morning, he finds the aspect of the country strangely altered, and asks his way of a man laboring in the fields. The man cannot understand what the king says, and it turns out that the night in Fairyland had lasted three hundred years, and and that the Saxons now ruled the land that had been Britain.

Here we have the meeting of two motives: the Sleeper motive and the visit to Fairyland motive. The story as it stands in Mapp is a slight thing; one sees, I think, that if it had fallen into the right hands it might have become a high romance.

Commander Bell, R. N., writing to a daily paper, makes a notable point as to the connection between malaria and the mosquito, discovered, so far as the West is concerned, by Sir Ronald Ross. He quotes Colonel Swayne, an African traveller of the 'eighties and early 'nineties.

The Somalis themselves denied that the sickness was caused by bad water, declaring that the real cause was the bites of mosquitoes. These pests are not generally present in eastern Somaliland, but are common at certain spots on the coast between Berbera and Zeila Harrar. They are also found near the Webbe, and when there the tribes who are not accustomed to mosquitoes have a great dread of these pests, believing malaria fever to be caused by them.

This is but one example among many of savage instinct anticipating science. The South American Indians discovered quinine as a specific in malaria: and ignorant old Englishwomen treated goitre with a particular kind of seaweed, containing iodine—though neither they nor anybody else of their period had heard of iodine. How did they do it; these savage Indians and illiterate Englishwomen? It is an interesting subject of speculation, which may be extended indefinitely. We do not yet know the process by which it was discovered that orange juice and port mingled make it a fit accompaniment to wild duck.

Dr. J. B. Baillie, presiding at the Empire University's Congress at Cambridge, has been committing himself to strange doctrines. He said that physical training and athletics must be subordinated to the main purpose for which a university existed. And as if this were not enough, he boldly, nay, brazenly, declared that "a university was not a sports club."

"Nice goings on!" as the song says. I am glad to know that Dr. Baillie was brought to book, promptly and sharply. Dr. Amami, Vice-Chancellor of Liverpool University, said that the ideas of our universities, and of the chairman (Dr. Baillie), came from the medieval ages, when Church doctrine taught abstinence. How thankful we are to be that we do not live in the medieval ages. And how jolly it must be at Liverpool University, where Rabelais' dream is realized, and *Fay ce que vouldras rouldras* is, doubtless, over the portals of the room where they read for the B.Sc. (Shipowning).

So the explanation of the Marie Celeste mystery will not stand. The Marie Celeste, it will be remembered, which was the ship which was so strangely found on the high seas with all things in perfect order, with a meal prepared, with no trace of affray or struggle, and yet derelict, without a man on board, with never a word to declare what strange fate had come upon the crew. A recent article in "Chambers's Journal" declared that the mystery resolved itself into an elaborate salvage swindle, and the information was said to have been taken from the confession of John Pemberton, on board the Dei Gratia, the ship which discovered the Marie Celeste.

But "Lloyd's List" has taken the explanation in hand. And "Lloyd's List" is not to be trifled with as to clearings and dates of sailings. "Lloyd's List" knows when the Dei Gratia cleared, when the Marie Celeste sailed; and it declares that the Pemberton story cannot be true. I am glad of it. I do not want to have the words and music (original notation) of the song that the syrens sing. The more mysteries the better.

The most wonderful story of the sea I know is a perfectly true one—in a certain sense. A certain captain of the Mercantile Marine, a Dane of origin, and of very great courage, indeed, so far as I can gather from his son-in-law, of a certain wildness of courage, once determined to sail in an open boat from Gibraltar to Florida. With him he had his son, a boy of twelve. Some days out from Gibraltar very foul weather was encountered, and the boat was in difficulties. Captain Andersen was without sleep for several days, and was on the verge of collapse. Suddenly a number of men climbed over the side and began to busy themselves in sailing the boat. They were dressed like Moors, they spoke among themselves a language which the captain took to be Arabic; one of them attracted his attention in a very particular manner. This man had an artificial leg, and the false limb ended in a square metal plate, which the captain observed glittered with the polish of much use. Well, this strange crew made everything ship shape and all atauto—I quote Captain Swasser—the gale abated, the crew went as they had come, over the side of the boat. The voyage ended happily.

Such was the story told by Captain Andersen, such was the story which appeared in the London Press of the day—I think it was about 20 years ago—such the story that the captain's son-in-law; adding that his father-in-law was convinced that he had been saved by a company of spirits. I was highly interested. I suggested that the captain's son, his companion on the voyage, should be questioned. This was done, and it seemed that the boy, now a young man had seen nothing of the enchanted Moors. Once or twice his father had sent messages by him to figures that the captain saw clearly; but, in the son's words, "there was nothing there."

Eighteen

August 1, 1926

We were discussing the Coal Strike the other day, as most of us have been discussing it at intervals for the last three months or so. I said:—

"But, after all, they—the colliers— have a horrible life."

Another man:—

"Well, I don't know. What is a horrible life? If you were obliged to live at the Hotel Glorieux—compulsory golf and auction bridge—and had to dance the Charleston every night at the Ham and Eggs Club, you would call that a horrible life, wouldn't you?"

I had to confess that he was right. I can imagine no life more horrible; quite allowing that to very many people it would seem a foretaste of Paradise. And that is what the other man was getting at. He was warning me that I must not make my notions of the horrible a rule for the miners of Tonypandy and Hetton-le-hole.

And I was reading, only the other day, a learned address delivered before the British Medical Association at Nottingham, in which the *conferencier* showed that, in one respect at all events, the collier is better off than many of those who pity him. The cancer death rate in colliery districts is about half that prevailing in such pleasant places as Hempstead, Kensington, Bath, and Oxford.

So the case of "The Chronicle of Cleophas" has been decided against Mr. Bligh Bond, and in favor of Miss Cummins, who wrote the text down. Many odd things struck me about the "Chronicle." In the first place, the style was very queer. There was an attempt to write archaic English; but the construction was of no known period. Modern phrases appeared here and there. The grammar was, frequently, ferocious: "I will wait here for ye" is an example. And why should the communicating spirit, contemporary of the Apostles, call this country of ours, "Anglia?" There were no Angles in Britannia in his day. He had heard of the Teutonic invasion? Then he would also have heard that the country has long been known as England.

In the course of the singular case, some reference was made to the British Israel Society. A week or two ago I mentioned their interesting derivation of "Saxon" from "Isaacson"; and a correspondent sends me an account of a meeting held under the auspices of the British-Israel

World Federation, at which some further striking etymologies were propounded. Thus:—

The main body of the tribe of Dan came in as the Danes, their jumping off place being Denmark. Part of the Judah people came in as the Jutes, their jumping off place being Jutland. The main body of the Israel people came into these islands as the Saxons or sons of Isaac. The prophesied reunion of the two kingdoms began to take place at the time of the formation of the Union Jack, or Union of Jacob. The Lion of Scotland, heraldry of Judah, and the Unicorn of England, the heraldry of Israel, were at the time brought together, and the title "United Kingdom of Great Britain," officially adopted.

"Union Jack" = "Union of Jacob" is as fine a thing (in its way) as Salisbury Cathedral. But one point puzzles me a good deal. The speaker insisted very strongly that "British" signified "Covenant man," being derived from the Hebrew words "Brith," meaning Covenant, and "ish," man. Now, "British" is derived from "Brython," the Celtic family represented now by the Welsh, the Bretons, and the men of Cornwall, as opposed to the Goidels, the ancestors of Irishmen, Scottish Highlanders, and Manxmen. And it is very certain that both these Celtic families are only related to Jutes, Saxons, and Danes as we and they are related to Greeks, Persians, and Italians. Moreover, to the best of my belief, the Celts came here before the dispersion of Israel.

M. Feuillerat, the author of "French Life and Ideals," praises the exquisite politeness of his countrymen, and gives, as an example, the case of the Duke of Bedford and the French eighteenth century nobleman. The English Duke was the host, and he promised his guest a glass of a very rare and curious wine. The Frenchman tasted the wine and emptied the glass, praising the drink in the highest degree. The Duke of Bedford tasted in his turn, uttered an exclamation of horror and loathing. There had been a mistake. The bottle contained castor oil. On this, an English critic comments that true politeness would have warned the Duke of Bedford as to the contents of the bottle.

I like the similar tale in "Peregrine Pickle" better. At the Banquet after the Manner of the Ancients the host announces that, not being quite clear as to the *nitron* of the ancient diners, he had used asafoetida in the soup instead. The French Marquis said that the soup was all together excellent, upon his word of honour. After the third spoonful he became very ill, and was taken home in his sedan-chair. But, let it be added, the German Baron finished his portion and asked for more.

I believe that Carp Boiled in Beer is the national Christmas dish of modern Germany.

There is room, I think for a fair compromise in the matter of the nineteen City churches which the Church Assembly and the Bishop of London wish to sell and destroy. In the good old days of the City it was common to celebrate some special mercy or deliverance by founding an annual sermon in commemoration; such, for example, is the Lion Sermon, which, I believe, is still preached. Well, why not endow an annual sermon to celebrate the destruction of the nineteen churches? It would be called, picturesquely, as I think, the Spikenard Sermon. The preacher would take as his text:—

"Then sayeth one of his disciples, Judas Iscariot. ... Why was not this ointment sold for three hundred pence and given to the poor?"

I believe that the money realized by the sale of the church sites in the City is destined for the most amiable objects.

The City authorities are opposed to the whole transaction, and have petitioned the House of Commons against it, with all their traditional solemnity and splendor. But the Lord Mayor and all his people are the devoted lovers of old things and old customs. The Court of Hustings must be the most ancient Court in the world, and an election at Guildhall, with its show of hands and demand for a poll is conducted on precisely the same principles as that famous election at Eatanswell— less the bribery and corruption.

Nineteen

August 8, 1926

Is the sun myth coming back again in the disguise of the seasonal myth? I have just been reading a highly ingenious and, in some ways, admirable essay on Hamlet. Mr. Percy Allen, the author of the essay, concludes that the citizens of Elsinore, who put up "The Taming of the Shrew," and not "Hamlet," to celebrate the five hundredth anniversary of their charter, desired to hint their disbelief in the connection between Hamlet and Elsinore. And Mr. Allen says that they were right.

The fable of "The Moody One"—the old actors' name for Hamlet—carries us back, he says, to the beginning of prehistoric man:—

The primeval savage, looking about him upon forces which he feared and misunderstood, was yet acute enough to recognise his dependence for material well-being upon a favorable succession of crops, and therefore with conciliatory intent towards nature—and, as we still do, holding imitation to be the sincerest form of flattery—began with simple ritual dances and miming plays to ape the round of the seasons. Gradually there developed in him a habit of personifying seasonal conflicts, and of fitting them to his folktales, until, with the advent of the great Hellenic age, the dramatic poets, Æschylus, Sophocles, and the rest, whose task it was to provide their nation's plays, found these elemental nature-figures and their stories already incorporated, consciously or unconsciously, into the heroic national legends, which were to form the Attic drama's central theme.

And so, we get along very pleasantly and easily. The personages of the Greek drama are "personifications of the nature battle between the seasons—Orestes being the winter, Clytemnestra the earth-mother, and Aegisthus the Sun"; and, finally, it is clear that Hamlet is, in reality, Orestes under another name. I am charmed by the theory; I don't think anything is better fun than learned ingenuity, and—I don't believe one word of it. In the first place; primitive man had no crops: he was a hunter. And I have lived in the days when Max Mueller taught us that the whole story of the Iliad was merely a sun-myth, that the great tale of Achilles is a description of the sun's march across the sky. We all believed Max, till another German, Schliemann, was impertinent enough to discover Troy, with all the evidence of its having been sacked and burned, as Homer tells us. And so, Mr. Allen gives us leave to hold that Hamlet was a Norse Prince, and that his tale and its broad outline was much as Shakespeare tells us.

...

Once on a time I knew an astrologer, a very ingenious young man. On one occasion he told me that he annoyed his father a good deal by writing to console him on the bad fall from his horse—that was to happen in a fortnight's time. And my friend told me that his father was crosser than ever when the accident happened as per prediction. Now, for this matter I have only the astrologer's word; but I remember very clearly how he told me of three several events that, as he said, had happened to me the week before his utterance; of which he could have had no knowledge, save from the stars. And, then, on the other hand, so far as I recollect, not a single star-gazer predicted the Great War, one of the hugest events in human history. Dr. Garnett, the skeptical and all-knowing, was a firm believer in astrology; but what do we know?

These reflections are provoked by the strange case of Mr. Matchett, who with the greatest determination and courage, recently rescued two women from a burning house in Maida Vale. And it turned out that the Maida Vale business was Mr. Matchett's third experience of fire. He jumped forty feet in his escape from a fatal fire at Baghdad, he rescued two children from a burning house at Maidenhead—and I should like to see his horoscope. If it does not indicate, very strongly, peril from fire; then Dominie Sampson was right, and Colonel Mannering was wrong.

Mr. Ellis Barker has been comparing the pre-industrial age with the present, in all respects vastly to the advantage of the latter. I suppose the dispute is one that will never be ended; some will always think with greater pleasure of a cavernous hearth with roaring logs flaming up it than of the most perfect system of central heating. But I believe Mr. Barker goes too far when he says that in pre-factory days the working masses inhabited "flimsy and unhealthy hovels made of lathes and pounded clay or loam covered with thatch." If these hovels were so flimsy, how is it that Londoners of the present day live in them in the summer—if they can get them? A really flimsy fifteenth, sixteenth, or seventeenth century house would have crumbled away long ago. Of course, when Mr. Ellis Barker points out that factory-made linoleums were unknown in the dark ages we have to hold up our hands and cry mercy.

It has been stated lately that the favorite carriage for the Gretna Green affairs of a hundred years ago was the "britska," "a four-wheeled open contrivance of graceful appearance, built for two (and the luggage), with a large hood, and a little seat at the back for the trusty service maid." Now, is this specification of the britska correct? I refer to an Immortal Work and find the following passage:—

She (Mary) appeared to have an original genius for making the right people give a lift in their carriages to the distressed; and regarding the Abbotstoke britzska as her own, packed in Mrs. Anderson and Fanny, in addition to all their own little ones, Meta thrusting Miss Bracy into the demi-corner for herself.

Now, there were three little ones, Gertrude, Aubrey, and Blanche. So here we have a britska (or britzska), holding three grown-ups and three children. Miss Bracy, who, it will be recollected, was a governess, no doubt sat in the maid's dickey; but poor Mrs. Anderson and Fanry, in the front seat, have been sadly crowded by the little ones. I hope it is unnecessary; but perhaps I had better add that the masterpiece cited is "The Daisy Chain."

There is no question now from any quarter as to the almost—or quite—unearthly beauty of the character of St. Francis, whose festival they are keeping at Assisi. But it is curious to note how the attitude of science has changed as to the mysterious Stigmata. Fifty years ago science said, "what a pity to tell outrageous lies about a good man: the Stigmata are, of course, impossible." To-day Stigmata—often of a quite mundane significance—are observed in the hospitals.

Twenty

August 15, 1926

It is interesting to find that the myth-making faculty still survives amongst us, and in a very curious and interesting form. In a way one is glad, I think, to know that it is so; the pity of it is that the latest addition to mythology is disfigured by so many ugly and foolish features.

Of course, the tale that I have in mind is the legend of Kitchener. I have been reading how the General's body has been recovered and brought home from some lonely Norwegian shore, and so far this is the latest chapter in the fable. But the legend began very soon after the disaster of the Hampshire, and in a different form. In its earliest shape, it told how Kitchener was not dead at all, but alive and a prisoner in Germany. It was said that his own relations knew that he was alive, and I believe that the tale in this guise held the field as late as 1920-21. But already, let it be remarked, there were intimations of the blackest treachery behind the story. I am not sure, but I'm inclined to think that it was held that the Admiralty had conspired with lubbers, unspecified, and that "Salome," a well-known dancer, and a mysterious Book kept in Germany had something to do with this black business.

Soon after this, the "spirits" took a hand in the affair. The survival of the great General was abandoned; the manner of his passing was described, and again, the blackest treasons and stratagems and spies were indicated as the means of Kitchener's death. But this once accomplished, the tale went on to show how Mary Queen of Scots told Lord Kitchener that Queen Victoria was helping King Edward over his portrait painting, instructing him in putting in the eyes. Finally, the latest legend deals out treason and villainy with a more lavish hand than any other version, builds the Hampshire in the eclipse, and rigs it with curses dark, and describes Kitchener's last moments on a desolate coast. Even there, if I remember, his faithful spy followed him; and now has been recovered—the Admiralty says the whole tale is a pack of lies from beginning to end. Well; it is our modern version of the Passing of Arthur, but one cannot help feeling that the telling of the older legend fell into happier hands.

It will be remembered that when Mrs. Todgers had shown the Miss Pecksniffs the view from the roof of Todgers's. Bailey junior lingered behind to walk upon the parapet, "contemplating with a delight peculiar to his sex and time of life any chance of dashing himself into small fragments." They have been having an epidemic of Bailey juniorism in Paris lately. A young man climbed up the face of a tall building in the Boulevard des Italiens. Another young man scaled the Eiffel Tower from the outside; climbed the southern Tower by Notre Dame, also from the outside. And the Alpinists are always busy; and, after all, they are nothing but Bailey juniors on a magnificent scale. It is one of the paradoxes of human nature, but it is certain that many men love peril for its own sake. The Arctic explorer, fitting out his ship, will have dozens, perhaps hundreds, of applicants for each vacancy on board. So many there are eager for certain misery and a chance of death.

In a story of De Maupassant's, the man coming home from his evening at the café is horrified to be met at his garden gates by his own furniture. Chairs and tables and bureaus, all the furniture of his house, pour down the drive and pass through the gates and vanish into the night. It was sometime later, I think, that the bereaved owner of the furniture met it all again, as the stock of a shop in a town in a remote part of France. There is no explanation: very few writers have the courage to refuse explanations. Life is usually profuse in explaining away strange incidents, explaining away at the same time all their interest. Thus in a true story from Paris we have De Maupassant's tale explained away and mangled.

Victor Hollmann, a Parisian dealer in antiques, married a widow with two sons. He began to have his doubts about the widow's loyalty; however, the pair went off last month for a motor tour in the provinces, leaving the house and the business in the charge of the two sons. But after a few days the dealer found he must pay a brief visit to Paris. He found his shop closed, his furniture deserted. All his domestic furniture was gone, his stock was gone. His two step sons had gone. He rushed back to Royan, where he had left his wife and the car. His wife had gone. The car had gone. So far magnificent; the ending is poor. The wife and the suspected lover were found at Nice, also the stock and the furniture. The guilty couple had hoped to furnish a boarding house, and, I suppose, to open an old curiosity shop. And so what should have been a noble tale ends scurvily in the police court.

It should be possible to make a very curious collection of unexplained tales. The best that occurs to me is Grimaldi's story of the return of his long-lost brother. Here it is not so much the actual circumstances that are strange. In the closing years of the eighteenth century, I dare say that many lads went to sea and remained unheard of for year after year. Sometimes, not always, they came back with money in their pockets. So far, Grimaldi's story of his brother has nothing strange about it; nor is it very remarkable that a well-dressed young fellow, who wonders about the purlieus of Drury-lane at midnight with a boastful air and a bag full of money, should disappear again, and this time for ever. The true strangeness lies in the manner in which the famous clown tells the tale, and his very evident doubt at one point in the story as to whether his brother had really returned at all. Indeed, there are moments when I doubt myself, I wonder whether this tale of the long-lost brother and his return is not the astounding—and veridical—history of an apparition.

Twenty-one

August 22, 1926

A searcher into secret things, writing to a newspaper, asks for light on Mrs. Nickleby's reference to the Thirsty Woman of Tutbury. It may be said, in satisfaction of this most reasonable desire, that for once Mrs. Nickleby was not wholly accurate. She should have said the Fasting Woman of Tutbury.

This lady, Ann Moore (or Peg), was born in humble circumstances in 1761. Her early career was not one of great austerity, but it was only in 1807 that she declared that she could live without food. The inhabitants of Tutbury, led by a Mr. Taylor, surgeon, watched her for sixteen days, and were convinced that she had neither eaten nor drunk anything for thirteen of them. The result of this manoeuvre was £250 for the Fasting Woman. Eventually, of course, she was found out and sent to prison for obtaining money by false pretences. But there is a more important point to be noted. Mrs. Nickleby had a vague notion that the Thirsty Woman of Tutbury might have gone to school with her grandmother. This could not have been. Ann Moore, "humbly asking pardon for all persons whom I have attempted to deceive and impose upon," and confessing "that I have occasionally taken sustenance for the last six years," duly delivered her confession. But she did so by her mark. It is, therefore, quite clear that she did not go to school with Mrs. Nickleby's grandmother. Indeed, supposing Mrs. Nickleby to have been born in 1780—a date for which I am prepared to contend—it is clear that the Fasting Woman, born in 1761, could not possibly have been a contemporary of Nicholas Nickleby's great-grandmother.

Amongst the things rare and strange and curious discussed at the meeting of the British Association, there was nothing queerer than Mr. E. G. Bowen's discourse of dark Welshmen, Calvinism, and consumption. There is a relish in seeing things apparently remote from one another related in spite of all; and this relish Mr. Bowen provided. It seems—I am the slave of his statistics—that the little "black" Welsh suffer sadly from tuberculosis when they live on the bare hills, but tend to become immune when they descend into the industrial valleys. The fair Welsh, on the other hand, flourish in the open air and die of consumption in the "works" and the mines.

And Mr. Bowen's explanation? The dark Welsh are emotional and given to attending revival meetings and singing festivals in crowded, unhealthy chapels. Afterwards they walk home long distances in the cold night air. Also, they are Calvinists; and Calvinism is fatalistic, and has a tendency to think of the human body as subject to corruption.

Well; of course a condensed report may have misrepresented Mr. Bowen; but his theory as it stands won't hold water. Why do the little black Welsh get better when they come down from the hills to Llanelly? They are still Calvinists, they are still revivalists, they are still addicted—hugely—to singing in parts. And are there not many of the Methodistiud Calfinaidd discipline amongst fair Welshmen? The real truth of the matter is quite remote from all this. The little black people pine on the hills and thrive in the industrial valleys because their original place was in caves and hollows under the earth. They are not Celts at all; they are the descendants of the aborigines; and probably the atmosphere of a Welsh mining village is not at all unlike that of the black, smokey holes under the hills where the fathers of these little people dwelt when the Celts, the fair Welshman, came from the Land of Summer. These were the people of iron, who subdued the people of stone, the cave-dwellers. So it is clear enough why the fair men pine away in the industrial towns. Their place is in the sunlight on the mountain, not in the smoky pits of Tonypandy.

There is something strangely moving in the account of the sheep of goodwill. Another sheep had fallen into a sunken water tank, and the good beast, her companion, ran to a chance passer-by and baaed loudly, and thus guided the human being to the tank. The gentleman who reports the tale says that, as an elderly man, he could not affect the rescue alone and went for help, and bitterly did the pious sheep reproach him for abandoning her friend, as she supposed. All ended happily. The sheep that had fallen into the pit was drawn out; and seeing that this was done, the faithful friend returned to her lamb. I do not know what St. Francis would have said of this. I almost think that he would have asked his "Sister Sheep" to pray for him. But one thing, I think, is pretty evident, if such a beast as a sheep, which has never stood in any relation of affection or familiarity with man, is capable of such devotion to another of the silly flock, we may safely disregard the sordid theories which make a dog's loyalty to his master a mere matter of calculated self-interest. The dog will stay by the master who has perished in the snow storm, will stay by him to the death. "Yes," say the sordid men, "because he has been taught that his master is the only being who can give him a bone." What did the sheep hope to get when her fellow was drawn out of the pit?

Judge Perry, I see, has included the Tichborne Claimant in his forthcoming book of "Vagabonds All." And I wonder whether the real truth about this extraordinary man will ever be known. He was not the verifiable Roger; there can be no doubt about that. But I think it is almost certain that he was a Tichborne, though an illegitimate one; it is even possible that he was the son of James Francis Tichborne and his wife, born before wedlock, and bestowed with the Ortons of Wapping. It is noteworthy that there had been old relations of some kind between the Tichbornes and the Wapping people; also that neither side ventured to call the Ortons as witnesses.

I do not know that Mr. A. E. Waite, the author of "The Secret Tradition in Alchemy," all together accepts the very interesting theory of Berthelot, the distinguished French chemist, as to alchemical origins. Berthelot held that the whole art of transmutation arose from a grotesque misunderstanding. A third-century papyrus gives a number of craft recipes for silvering and gilding metals. This, Berthelot conjectures, fell into barbarous hands in a later age, and the recipe for making iron look like gold was taken to be a recipe for turning iron into gold. It may have been so, but this is not so picturesque as the thesis put forward in a nineteenth-century book called "A Suggestive Inquiry into the Hermetic Mystery." Here the theory was that alchemy is the account, in symbolical language, of the process by which humanity may be raised to Divinity.

Twenty-two

August 29, 1926

"When all is said, the fact remains that Don Quixote is what American slang calls 'bug house.'" True, indeed; and when all is said, the fact remains that Mr. Pickwick was what American slang calls a "sucker." Not a "Rube," nor by any means a "Hayseed," since Mr. Pickwick's occupations before his famous tour are understood to have been urban, but he was decidedly a sucker, and I am inclined to think that we should do Mr. Pickwick no great injustice if we call him "Mr. Easy Mark of Marksville."

Strange to relate, the sentence that I have quoted occurs in an article in "The Times" concerned in the first place with "Don Quixote," in the second place with "Pickwick," and generally with the picturesque romance. To continue in the American vein, I think I may say that in the opinion of "A. B. W.," the writer, neither of the three propositions cut any sort of ice. Don Quixote, as we have seen, was bughouse, and is only tolerated on account of Sancho Panza's proverbs; "Pickwick," in like fashion is saved by Sam Weller and his Wellerisms; and the picaresque plot, "a hotchpotch of miscellaneous adventures, with no unifying bond, save that they all happen to the same persons," strikes "A. B. W." "as the worst possible of plots for fiction." Well, the Don was rather nobly wild than mad, and Hamlet shows a great spirit distracted by the wickedness of all about him—"to be wroth with those we love Doth work like madness in the brain." Still; each age has its own taste. We are repelled by the insanity of Don Quixote and Hamlet; let us take refuge in studies of sore old maids, with sores on their legs, and sores on their souls. But it's a queer world, as Miss Knag said: and "A. B. W.'s" criticism is a Queer Thing which well becomes it.

The story of the Perfect Murder at Harrogate—let us assume its truth for the moment—seems to suggest some curious questions in the philosophy of crime and punishment. Scotland Yard has received an anonymous confession, neatly typed. The writer declares that twelve years ago he had a grudge against a man, and resolved to kill him. The man who was to murder and the man who was to be murdered were both staying at an hotel at Harrogate. The latter suffered from acute heart disease, and one night the writer of the confession came to the victim's room. The villain pointed a revolver at his enemy's head, and told him that one of them must die. He then produced two packets containing white powder. One of these packets, he declared, contained arsenic, the other chalk. Each was mixed in a glass of water: The wretched man, the revolver at his head, was told to choose—and drink. He did so, and fell down in his death agony. The "murderer" told the hotel people that his friend had died in a heart attack; there was an inquest, and a verdict accordingly.

There was no arsenic in either packet, according to the confession. And, as it is said, the police have discovered that a man did die on the date named, at Harrogate twelve years ago, and found that a small quantity of chalk was found in his stomach at the post-mortem examination. And, here is the point: supposing all this to be true, and supposing the writer of the confession identified and put to the bar, can justice find him guilty of murder and proceed to hang him by the neck until he is dead?

The question seems to me full of difficulties. Morally, all is clear. The writer of the confession, deliberately and of malice aforethought, uttered certain words and performed certain actions which, he was convinced, would result in the death of the man he hated. In the high court of final justice, he is an undoubted and most devilish murderer. But is he a murderer in English—or human—law? For, be it observed, he was guilty of no violence against the body of his enemy. He uttered threats in menaces, certainly; and to threaten is, I believe, an indictable offense; but it is far from being a capital one. Then, again by threats, he induced his victim to swallow a fluid, which (as he caused him falsely to believe) might or might not contain a fatal dose of arsenic. I do not know whether such a course of conduct be indictable; but the offense, if any, is, again, certainly not capital. For, it will be noted, the villain of the tale committed no assault on the body of his enemy; but merely attacked his soul. Does our criminal law recognize the existence of the soul?

If the answer is in the affirmative, then the man who rushes into a house with the news: "Your son has hanged himself in the shrubbery!" may swing for it. It will be necessary, no doubt, to establish malice, also to prove that the murderer was aware that his victim's heart was likely to be dangerously affected by a sudden shock; then the verdict of the jury must be "guilty." And I do not see that this verdict could be affected by any considerations as to the truth or falsity of the death-dealing announcement.

...

The Six Jolly Fellowship Porters has always been a favorite tavern of mine. Many a pleasant evening have I spent in Cosy—or was it Snug?—watching Bob Gliddery burning the sherry, or receiving my portion of flip from Miss Abbey's own hands. Consequently, from force of association, I was sorry when the Guild, or Mystery, or Company of the Fellowship Porters was dissolved, some time ago. And now they have been selling a silver cup, which once belonged to this odd Fellowship, a cup given to the Guild in 1637 by a Merchant Taylor of the day. I am always sorry when these old songs come to an end. It is hard work hauling loads of coal and corn, fruit and fish up from the ship's side by the black wharf passages; and perhaps it did the weary porter no harm to think of his Brotherhood, with its silver cups, its yearly service at St. Mary-at-Hill, its high feasts, its nosegays of flowers. And, no doubt, it cheered a porter to remember that he belonged to the Corne Porters grade in the Mystery, and was thus a Dandy and a White Mouse; not a Dirty or a Smelly, handler of coals, potatoes, or fish. And, on the other hand, if a Dandy died or avoided the Fellowship, there was always a chance of a Senior Dirty taking his place. It seems to me that hard work must have been sweetened by this mixture of dignity, festivity, good-tempered whimsicality. Trade unions are admirable institutions, but perhaps they have something to learn from the departed Fellowship Porters.

Twenty-three

September 5, 1926

Mr. A. G. Bradley says in his "Exmoor Memories" that the whole business of the Doones was the pure invention of Blackmore. There were never such people, and there was no tradition of them in the neighbourhood. An old Exmoor rector told Mr. Bradley that he had never heard of such folk, and more, the rector had never heard of Blackmore.

Well, in a sense, I should have been glad if this tale had been true. "Lorna Doone" is a noble book, though somewhat over-lyrical, and the author's credit would have been all the higher if it could be shown that he had not only invented the story of "Lorna Doone," but also the tradition on which the story is based. But, of course, Mr. Bradley is all wrong, and his ancient rector did not know what he was talking about. A correspondent of "The Times" puts in evidence that cannot be avoided or denied. He cites a Devonshire Directory published in 1857, twelve years before the appearance of "Lorna Doone," in which, under the heading of "Brendon," it is stated that "the district abounds with legends about robbers, called 'The Doones of Bagworthy.'" So, in the decisive, if disgusting, Scottish idiom: "Let that flea stick to the wa'!" The existence of the Doone legend before the publication of "Lorna Doone" is definitely and finally established.

There is, I believe, an interesting hypothesis to the effect that these Bagworthy brigands were, in reality, a Celtic remnant, driven into the wildest winds by the Saxon invasion, and holding out in their valley, at first, perhaps, as patriots, and then and ever after as pure thieves, till they were smoked out as a nuisance towards the end of the seventeenth century. The theory is attractive, and maybe true, likely enough. But I am interested by the minor point: the nescience of Mr. Bradley's rector. I have long been aware that there is a whole world of country life of which neither the rector, the squire, the lawyer, nor the doctor have the faintest notion. I remember when I was a boy, a countryman instructing me as to the necessity of gathering medicinal herbs under certain planets—one of these planets was called Juniper! And I am very sure that my father, the rector, would have laughed at the notion that his parishioners were believers in astrology. And some thirty-five years ago a West-Country cloth manufacturer published a very admirable book on the Evil Eye. He showed that in the 'eighties, clay images, made after a horrible and most ancient recipe, were still being pierced with nails and pins in Somersetshire cottages. But I am very certain that the Somersetshire rectors had never heard that tale as they went on their pastoral visitations.

And while we are on this topic, I may say that I am looking forward with some curiosity to "The History of Witchcraft and Demonology," by Mr. Montague Summers, which is to appear in the course of this autumn. There are all sorts of puzzles in this matter which are waiting for an answer. For example: Was there any such a thing, in historic times, as the Witches' Sabbath? Is there anything to be said for Payne Knight's contention, that it was a relic of the pagan, priapic cultus persisting in secret in Christian times? Or, was the Witches' Sabbath the relic of an older world than the Roman: the Western equivalent to the secret societies of the African negroes, in which the Medicine Man—the "Black Man" of the witch stories—hideously arrayed in demoniac guise, presides over the assembly? When and where was the last Sabbath held in England? If Mr. Summers answers these questions, I shall be grateful to him.

The debate as to the pronunciation of Cirencester is interesting. It seems pretty certain that the name should be pronounced "Sisester" or "Siseter"; or, the speech of the country folk, "Ziseter." The analogies of Gloucester, Bicester, Worcester, support this view; and it is probable that the literal pronunciation, "Cy-ren-ces-ter" is due to the enthusiasm of people who had learned, a hundred years ago or more, how to spell, and were resolved to utilise their new learning. We speak now of the Peninsula of Gower, pronouncing the word as it is spelt. But, "Leveson Gore," and "King Uriens of Gore"—that is Gower—appears in the "Morte d'Arthur." And so the name "Barclay" no doubt gives the proper pronunciation of "Berkeley," and I suspect that the accent was originally on the last syllable.

An American friend of mine arrived on these shores fortified with the knowledge that Southwark is pronounced "Suthock." In the course of his stay in London, he told a taxi-driver to take him to "Suthock Cathedral." The man stared at him in deep perplexity. "Suthock Cathedral," repeated my friend. Then the solution dawned on the puzzled driver. "Oh, you mean South Wark," he said, making "wark" rhyme with "stark." And, I suppose, the place has not been called thus for a thousand years.

...

There are latent mysteries in all things, even in those which seem most devoid of mystery. Here is an example of this great truth. The great railway companies, you must know, print a document called a "Daily Stock Return," and the following are amongst the items in the stock: Minks, mites, macaws, serpents, crocodiles, totems, beavers, beetles, pythons, scorpions, hydras, bloaters, tadpoles, butterflies, crickets, melons, and monsters. No; I shall make no attempt at explanation. A few weeks ago, I tried my best to explain the terms "Perfect Ashlar" and "Children of the Widow," and I was told in some quarters that I did not make myself clear. I was a good deal hurt.

Arthur Machen

Twenty-four

September 12, 1926

There is something curiously interesting and suggestive in the recent discovery of the straight paved way at York. This way, it appears, is in line with another paved road beyond the city, the purpose and age and objective of this road having been a mystery till very recent times. The latest opinion is that these straight cobble-paved tracks are pre-Roman, nay, prehistoric. They are said to be primitive trade routes, along which the remote pedlar carried his pack of salt and right Brandon flints to settlements of the caves or the lakes.

This is highly curious, as I say, but the most impressive circumstance to me is the straightness of these prehistoric tracks. And the point is that modern man is only just returning to the sound, practical common sense that ruled the world before the dawn of history; and for long afterwards. The pre-Celtic pedlar went by a straight road; the Celts, no doubt, having taught him his place, sent their bronze and amber and iron by the track of flints and salt; and when the Roman legions came, whether they used the ancient ways or made new ones, were marched in as straight a line as might be. And I was reading only the other day of the typical Roman town—Verona, I think—how it was laid out on the strictest rectangular principles. There was the broad main street, First-avenue we may call it, and from it went off, at regular intervals, First-street, Second-street, Third-street, and so on. A modern New Yorker would have felt absolutely at home in ancient Verona; while the torturous Londoner of fifty or five hundred years ago would have been ill at ease. And now look at Kingsway and the new motor roads.

And if one thinks of it, this contrast between antiquity, and the medieval world, and the age that is now upon us holds in other regions. The classic temple was a calm, rectangular, ordered building: Canterbury Cathedral seems to have grown, a living thing, out of the earth. The Roman letter A was just A, and nothing else: The Lombardic A of the Middle Ages might, very likely, turn itself into a rose tree. Now we have got back our plain honest A; and as for Mr. Chesterton's rolling English road, we are straightening it up finally. Once there was a winding, climbing lane in the West. On its high banks, all green growths and flowers mingled, above it dwarf oaks joined their branches from either side. Now, that lane is as straight, and sensible, and bare as a railway cutting. Give us time, and we shall be as practical as bees and ants.

...

There has been some discussion lately as to the custom of applauding at concert. It is pointed out that the habit of beating the hands together because you think that the man at the piano has played Bach or Beethoven very well, is utterly irrational. That is, no doubt, absolutely true; but is not the thing applauded as irrational as the applause? What rational, that is, practical ground can be discovered for the, more or less, measured noise that we call music? It seems to me that music is on the same plane as poetry, painting, sculpture, architecture, considered as the art of building beautifully: they are all irrational together. The fact is that, untold ages ago, a mammal went mad and thereby became man. The prehistoric man, who etched the picture of the reindeer on the reindeer bone, had "got'em." Or, if we reject this hypothesis, we shall find ourselves committed to theories which are utterly repugnant to science: to the science of yesterday.

For the last few weeks, I have been staying in a part of Britain where the architectural curiosity called the Squint can be very adequately studied. A squint is an opening in the chancel wall, so that the people in the side aisle, or some of them, may obtain a view of the High Altar. And here you have in stone a clear view of two strongly opposed theories of Christian worship; the old and the new. At Gumfreston Church, Pembrokeshire, the region which I have in mind, the chancel is divided from the nave by a solid stone wall, only pierced in the centre by a small rounded doorway. You will see an exactly similar arrangement at the Greek Church of Hagia Sophia, in the Moscow-road, Bayswater. Here, the central door is half glazed, so that the altar can be seen, but as the more sacred part of the service begins, a black veil falls, and the altar is hidden. And I have no doubt that, originally, a curtain was drawn across the doorway at Gumfreston, when the priest began the Canon of the Mass.[1]

The old view was that the central portion of Divine Liturgy should be a hidden mystery. The new view is that the High Altar and those things which are done there should be supremely visible; this theory may be seen in action at Westminster Cathedral, the Brompton Oratory, and St. Alban's, Holborn. The medieval Squint represents the transition from the old way to the new.

---

1 The Gumfreston church in Wales was a model for the "Mass of the Sangraal" in Machen's *The Great Return* (1915).

Twenty-five

September 26, 1926

Within the last few weeks a number of paleolithic axes have been found near Norwich. These axes, it is declared, were exquisitely shaped by men who lived about 100,000 years ago, and the conclusion is drawn that the makers of these axes were of a much higher type than the Neanderthal race which succeeded them.

The ascent of man, then, has not been continuous. There have been lapses: some of them, perhaps, of a terrific character. One such lapse is indicated by the very startling pronouncement of professor Max Westenhöfer, Director of the Pathological Museum of Berlin University. We have learned from the professors of old time that the human race is descended from apish ancestors; now this new professor declares that the anthropoid apes are descended from prehistoric man—and are superior to them in every respect save in the small matter of brains. According to Professor Westenhöfer, certain prehistoric men took to climbing, and also to nut-eating. Their arms grew stronger, their jaws also, by these exercises, thereby the blood supply to the brain was diminished and men became apes. And another point from the startling professor: the first reptiles, he declares, walked erect, like men. Here is happy news for Dayton, Tennessee.

Two Indian students, it is alleged, went the other day into a boot shop and asked for brown shoes. An argument arose as to the color of the shoes, and, according to the tale, one of the Indians, remarking that he did not like it, hit the manager of the shop hard with his walking-stick, so hard that the manager had to be taken to the hospital.

The rights and wrongs of the case—if there is a case—do not, and must not, concern us; but what an admirable opening for Mr. Sherlock Holmes, whom Sir Arthur Conan Doyle is benevolently reviving. We are not commenting on what happened or did not happen in fact; but in fiction we can see quite clearly that this sudden anger over a shade of brown leather was assumed. I am inclined to think that a plot of the "Moonstone" type is indicated.

It was "Observator," I think, who commented in last week's *Observer* on the singularity of the excuse proffered recently by a man of Newton Abbott, who refused to live with his wife. He said he would not live with her because she practiced witchcraft. Possibly, the Newtonian was a humbug; but possibly, also, he was quite sincere. As I pointed out in this column a few weeks ago, the belief in witchcraft still lingers in quiet places. It is thirty-five years, I think, since a woman in Ireland was burned alive by her husband, friends and relations standing around and consenting to the deed. The woman was not charged with being a witch; but he was quite sure that she was a fairy changeling. I do not know what horrible doctors in magic he had consulted, but the poor woman was burned at her own hearth, and then her husband sallied forth and went up a track on some black and desolate mountain in the neighbourhood. In his hand he bore a knife; bound by a leather thong to a white horse, and he must cut the thong, and his wife should be restored to him. But here something went wrong with the witch-doctor's medicine; and the man was sentenced to fourteen years' imprisonment.

Dean Inge, perhaps, would say: "What can you expect of a neolithic race?" But Balham is rather of the brick than the stone age; and the police had to be called out over a ghost at Balham a week ago. There is a house, it seems, in that happy suburb, so far lonely that it stands in its own grounds. It has been unoccupied for nearly two years. Before that a woman lived there for fifty years. There seems nothing very remarkable in any of the circumstances; but 500 Balhamites assembled in front of the house, and some of them declared that they had seen figures in white flitting past the windows. Then constables made a thorough search of the building—and found nothing.

I do not think we need take this particular instance of haunting very seriously; but on the general question, what do we know?

"'Talking of ghosts,' " he said: 'It is wonderful that five thousand years have now elapsed since the creation of the world, and still it is undecided whether or not there has ever been an instance of any person appearing after death. All argument is against it; but all belief is for it.' "

Thus the Doctor; and, as usual, it is well said, save that I do not see how there can be any argument, either way, as to the mighty possibilities of the other world. There may be no such world at all; but at any rate, supposing its existence, we know nothing about it. The Society for Psychical Research has some named and dated cases of apparitions which appear to be convincing, but, best of my recollection, these were appearances of persons at the moment of death. Has the society any sure evidence of post-mortem phantasms—that is, of veritable ghosts?

...

"The beautiful does not exist in objects, but is seen by you in them." This is a very new version of "Beauty lies in the eye of the beholder"; and may we say, with all respect, that both the old and the new aphorisms are false? Let us suppose a sentence in cypher exhibited to three people. The first pronounces it a random huddle of letters, without sense or significance. The second reads it with ease: "Tom has the mumps, but Aunt Jane says she cannot put off her visit to Stow-on-the-Wold, as the Dickensons have made their arrangements." Very well; but the third man sees that here we have a cipher within a cipher: that Tom and his mumps, Aunt Jane, the Dickensons, and Stow-on-the-Wold are not what they seem. The real message relates to Chinese politics, and the supply of machine-guns to Yang, or Wang, or Fang. But we must not say that the meaning of the sentence was not contained in it, only in the mind of the third man.

Twenty-six

October 3, 1926

Savages are the most logical of men—if you will only grant their premises. Last week I told the story of the unhappy Irish woman who was set by her husband on the fire because she was a changeling, and I confess that the proceeding seemed to me not only inhuman, but unreasonable, silly as well as cruel. But an obliging and most interesting Irish correspondent puts me right on this point. "The belief," she says, "is universal that any abnormal child or invalid is a fairy changeling, and if ill-treated the fairies will take it back. A cousin of my own, daughter of a County Cork baronet, was put on the shovel and held over the fire, because she was sickly. She grew up a fine, strong woman."

The reasoning, you see, is faultless. The fairies will not bear their kinsfolk, changelings, to be harshly used, and so will take them back to their place under the hills. But if the changeling goes back, then the human being must go back also, the exchange must be carried out fairly. It is perfectly reasonable, if you grant that first premise, that an invalid is a fairy changeling.

I have been reading with interest the argument as to the propriety of the sentence "The King goes to Scotland next Thursday." I should defend it against those who would substitute "will go" for "goes," on the ground that it is a witness for the Everlasting Now. Time is, after all, only one of the many illusions in which we are forced to believe.

Thus the judicious Harris—"a sound, sullen scholar," though a prig, according to Johnson—in his "Hermes: A Philosophical Inquiry Concerning Universal Grammar":—

"But if *no Portion* of Time be the object of *any Sensation*; farther, if the Present *never* exist; if the Past be *no more*; if the Future be not *as yet*; and if these are all the parts out of which Time is compounded; how strange and shadowy a being do we find it? How nearly approaching to a perfect Non-entity."

And the author goes to cite certain Greek philosophers (of whom few of us have ever heard), who declare that Time has its being in the soul alone, and in no other place.

We were discussing a little while ago the Doones of Bagworthy, and the question as to whether they had any existence outside the brain of Blackmore. Mr. A. G. Bradley tells me that he is still inclined to doubt the actuality of the Doones. He thinks it is likely enough that such a wild as Exmoor harboured rogues and robbers, but he doubts whether these robbers, granting their existence, were of the slightest interest. Very likely not, till Blackmore made them interesting.

A curious light is shed on the question by a correspondent of "Notes and Queries." Mr. W. Courthope Forman, who says that a serial story, called "The Doones of Exmoor," was published in "The Leisure Hour," in September-October, 1863. The tale is highly conventional and transpontine, but the assault on the Doone stronghold is described, and there are references to Faggus and his wonderful steed. It is conjectured that this blood-and-thunder tale gave Blackmore hints for the construction of "Lorna Doone." But I think we may fairly conclude that there was a tradition of a nest of bad men somewhere in the Exmoor wilds; a tradition which was demonstrably antecedent to "Lorna Doone."

But the problem of the origins of romance is often a perplexed and difficult matter. To take a far higher instance than "Lorna Doone": so great an authority as Professor Saintsbury—writing, it is true, years ago—declared that he could find no evidence for the Celtic source of the Grail Romances; indeed, the Welsh origins suggested by the late Principal Rhys were singularly futile. However, the Celtic sources of the Romances are to be found: but only in unlikely places, and after a fragmentary sort.

On the face of it, one would be apt to think that chess was a later and elaborated form of draughts. It is curious, but this is not the case. The Romans played draughts; the explorers of ancient things have recently found draughtsmen in a Roman fort at Bainbridge, Wensleydale. But, far as I am aware, there is no evidence that chess was known in Europe before the age of the Crusades.

Last week's *Observer* dealt faithfully with a gentleman who has sent himself to the emendation of the text of Shakespeare: changing, for example, a famous passage into:

> We are of such matter
> As makes a dream, and all of are little life
> Is finished by a sleep.

But this critic is not even original. He was anticipated by Mr. Curdle. That gentleman, it will be remembered, had written a pamphlet on the character of the Nurse's deceased husband in "Romeo and Juliet," with an inquiry whether he had really been a "merry man" in his lifetime. or whether it was merely his widow's affectionate partiality that induced her so to report him. And, in addition, Mr. Curdle had proved that, by altering the received mode of punctuation, "one of Shakespeare's plays could be made quite different, and the sense completely changed." I find in this last theory a rich foretaste of Baconianism.

A very singular subject is explored in "The Divining Rod," by the late Sir William Barrett and Theodore Besterman. I think that the fact of "dowsing," of smelling out water by supernormal means, is fairly established by the authors. But, of course, the rod, the forked twig used by Dowsers, has nothing vital to do with the process. Certain people, it seems proved, have a sixth sense—Mr. Besterman calls it "cryptesthesia," or hidden perception—which tells them that sometimes water, sometimes metals, are present. This sense—here is the curious point—communicates not with the mind, but with the muscles, causing a contraction, a kind of shudder. It is this muscular contraction which is registered by the twitching of the rod in the dowser's hands. It may be noted that other kinds of occult perception are announced by a tremor, or shudder, of the whole frame.

Twenty-seven

October 10, 1926

The case of Eleonore Zugun is a strange one. She is a Roumanian girl of thirteen. She was discovered in a lunatic asylum and was brought to England by the Countess Wassilko-Serecki. And the special correspondent of the "Daily News" says that while Eleonore was playing with some toys that she had brought her:

"Suddenly I noticed a small object falling seemingly from the ceiling onto Mr. Price's shoulder and then to the ground. Mr Price picked it up off the ground and examined it.

"It was a piece of white painted metal, smaller than a postage stamp, and shaped like the letter L."

This took place at the National Laboratory of Psychical Research, South Kensington. Eleonore was being "tested" at the top of the building. The small object was an L; it was found to be missing from a box of such letters (used for notices) kept in a cupboard on the ground floor, five stories below the room of the test.

And it only remains to be said that we have here either an ingenuously-planned piece of trickery or else an extraordinary manifestation of an extraordinary power.

Some years ago I did my best to investigate a Poltergeist, who was causing great trouble in a small house in a northern suburb of London. Coals came through windows, china was smashed, objects flew about the rooms. My investigations led me to no sure conclusion—I think the only person who could investigate the Poltergeist would have to be a member of the family with open eyes and an open mind—but it is noteworthy that, soon after the strange occurrences, one of the children of the house, a boy of eleven or twelve, became subject to epileptic fits. It may be irrelevant; but I cannot help comparing his epilepsy with Eleonore Zugun's alleged lunacy.

It is interesting to set beside these adventures a strange circumstance related in "Pot-Pourri Mixed by Two"; the authors being the late Mrs. Earle and Miss Ethel Case. Miss Case is responsible for what follows:—

"A curious thing happened to a friend of mine living in the country. She was going to London on a visit, and packed a small brown card-case carefully in a jewel-box; this she distinctly remembered doing. On leaving the house, the butler handed her a bag which she is in the habit of using when travelling, which contained a card-case, and she thought at once that she would use that one and not the other she had packed. She was in London a few days, and my brother met her to bring her down to stay with us. At Waterloo they got out at once into a first-class carriage, as the train was already at the platform. To her amazement, on the corner seat, was the identical brown card-case containing her cards which she had packed at the bottom of her trunk before she left home, and never seen since. She had travelled up from the country in a third-class carriage."

To me this affair is far more confounding than the L of Eleonore Zugun. It is an intolerable mystery.

At one of the Johnsonian gatherings, "much enquiry" was made concerning a gentleman who had just left the company. Johnson observed that "he did not care to speak ill of any man behind his back, but he believed the gentleman was an attorney." The race of the black-coated has always been a butt for gibes and jeers; the parson, the doctor, and the lawyer have been the subjects of ill jests for ages, and the attorney, perhaps, has fared the worst of all. On the journey to Bath in Smollett, the Boastful Captain—who in a happier hour became Dowler—said that there was nothing he did not dare. A meek little attorney in the coach objected—I quote from memory—"You dare not call me a rogue, since an action for slander would lie and I should recover." "I may not dare to call you a rogue," retorts the Captain, "but I dare think you one, damme!"

And the old joke is still alive. At the recent meeting of the Law Society, Mr. Ralph Tredgold told his fellow lawyers that on a recent visit to France he had met an American gentleman who said he knew London well. "When I asked if he knew Lincoln's Inn Fields, replied: 'Oh, yes, I have often passed Lincoln's Inn Fields, and have thought what a nest of thieves it is!'"

Some years ago the staff of a daily paper were discussing a rather promising murder that had been reported from Scotland.

"I think we ought to cover the inquest," said the news editor.

"There will be no inquest," I remarked.

"Nonsense," observed the news editor, tartly enough. "There must be an inquest."

"No," I maintained, "The Procurator Fiscal will just precognosce the case."

There was no answer to this—I suppose a far-off recollection of something in Sir Walter—but I was reminded of it the other day, in reading the recent proceedings in the Seafield Peerage Claim. Counsel for the plaintiff "asked his lordship to sustain the minute of abandonment and to discharge the diet of proof," but the counsel for the defense "maintained that the appropriate decree was one of absolution," and in the end, Lord Moncreiff "pronounced a decree of absolvitor." It is a rich language. I remember reading of a case in which a Scot was prosecuted for perjury—his evidence in the precognition of a case had differed considerably from his testimony at the trial. But the diet was deserted, and the panel practically assoilzied.

A good instance of the prophetic dream comes from St. Leonards. Miss Mary Douglas Hart, of that town, dreamed one night that an airplane fell into the sea, and that the pilot climbed out of the cockpit and waded ashore. The next morning Miss Hart was telling her sister about her odd dream, when the noise of an airplane was heard. The two looked out, and there, before their eyes, was the airplane falling into the sea, and presently, the pilot wading ashore.

Now, was Flight-Sergeant Payne, the pilot in question, beset by anticipation or foreboding of disaster the night before? We have no evidence to this effect; the journey was a short one—Folkestone the starting point—and the cause of the fall was sudden engine trouble. So I think we may say that Miss Hart's dream was an example of the prophetic as distinguished from the telepathic faculty. An event which had not happened was presented to her as happening. Here again we have a hint of that Everlasting Now which we discussed from another point of view last week.

Twenty-eight

October 17, 1926

We are, most of us, I suppose, under the impression that America is in all respects much more modern, advanced, progressive than England. We think, not without complacency, of our country as the home of the old ways, old customs, even of old superstitions; of America as too rich, too busy, too practical to have time for our ancient habits and beliefs. But we are mistaken in this. In the October number of the ever entertaining and informing "American Mercury," the Editor, Mr. H. L. Mencken, reviewing a book called "Folk Beliefs of the Southern Negro," says that the whites of the Southern states are as credulous as the blacks.

"It is highly probable," says Mr. Mencken, "that, outside the towns, at least nine-tenths of the poor whites of the South still believe in witches, and devote a great deal of time and energy to dodging them. This is certainly true in my own State of Maryland, which is relatively enlightened. In its Southern counties, adjacent to the intellectual cesspool of Washington, and on the pious Eastern Shore, ghosts and hobgoblins are still as real to the peasants, white and black, as they were to the villages of the Middle Ages. Every yokel, if he has not actually seen a ghost, knows someone who has, and has himself seen a black cat with fire coming out of its eyes, or a horse without a head, or a dog with two. ... The Southern rustic knows nothing of fairies, and can't imagine a benign spirit. The powers of the air are all evil, and every encounter with them is full of dangers. ... The kindly mythology that the early settlers brought from the Old World has been obliterated, and there remains only a legend of demons, goblins, and fiends."

It is only just to know that the fairies of the Old World were not always little people of unblemished character. The Celtic fairies were something very like fiends, and, in Mr. Mencken's phrase, a good deal of time and energy was devoted to dodging them. To this day, many houses within a few miles of Belfast have the mountain ash flourishing before their doors, not to look pretty, but to keep out the fairies. And less than fifty years ago a Monmouthshire farmer told me that a spray of may blossom, put on the threshold, guarded a house from the incursion of the People.

Eleonore Zugan, of whom we spoke last week, is supposed to

exhibit stigmatic marks, in addition to her Poltergeist accomplishments. From the photographs of the girl which have been reproduced in the newspapers, I should be inclined to diagnose nettlerash, or possibly eczema. Not that I am disputing, for a moment, the existence of the stigmata. In certain cases, strong emotion registers itself, as it were, on the body in visible form. A medical text-book relates the case of the lady who thought she saw her child's hand crushed by the fall of a heavy window-sash. As it happened, the child drew its fingers away just in time. But the mother fainted, and when she was restored it was observed that the fingers of one of her hands were grievously swollen and inflamed; in exactly the condition which they would have exhibited if they were crushed by the heavy sash.

Here we have a typical case of the stigmata; and, to return for a moment to our witches, is it not possible that there were—that there still are, for that matter—people with the power of projecting such an emotional shock against their fellows, sometimes with strange and dreadful results? The wounds on the lady's hands were "all imagination." And, by the way, Coventry Patmore, I remember, has a striking passage showing that the things which are most fervently to be desired, the things which are most fervently to be abhorred, are "all imagination." It is only the creatures below us in the scale of being, the animals, who live by and in actuality.

It is strange how the ages impinge on one another. A week or so ago a gypsy centenarian, oddly named Plato Buckland, died and was buried at Marlow. The rites of our age and of our religion were performed, no doubt, in the local cemetery; but afterwards the old man's children, grandchildren, great grandchildren, solemnly burned his caravan and all his possessions in a chalkpit near the town, the place of his encampment.

It is Mr. Chesterton, I think, who bids us be wary of inferring too much from such a custom: our descendants, as he says, would be very wrong if they inferred from our funeral customs a belief on our part that the dead eat lilies and orchids. Yet, on the other hand, we might find it difficult to give a clear account of our reasons for decking graves with flowers. Probably the Bucklands burned old Plato's goods and chattels because it had always been a custom for their tribe to do so; but I suppose that, in the beginning, the dead man's material belongings were consumed in order that they might become spiritual belongings in the spirit world. So Irish peasants at a funeral break their clay pipes and throw the pieces into the grave—that the dead man's ghost may have ghostly pipes to smoke.

It is noteworthy that in ancient Egypt and in modern Northamptonshire this principle did not and does apply. The various objects in Pharaoh's tomb were whole, not shattered; and in the Northamptonshire village, when a lover of tinned salmon died, they put an unopened tin of that delicacy in his coffin. Afterwards, it is true, they realised that the tin opener had been forgotten, but that necessary instrument was placed in the coffin of a relative who died soon afterwards. The village argued that the two had always been great friends and were sure to meet.

Arthur Machen

Twenty-nine

October 24, 1926

When Sancho Panza, Lord of the Island of Barataria, sat down to feast, Dr. Pedro Recio de Agüero, of Tirteafuera, physician in ordinary to the Governor, waved his wand, and dish after dish was borne away before the unhappy Governor could taste of any. The fruit was too moist, the spiced dish way too hot, the birds were unwholesome, the olla devoid of nourishment. This was a joke to Cervantes and his readers and to many generations of their successors. But such a tale would be no joke if told to-day. The doctor would have a "diet," and those who followed it would look upon the rest of humanity as almost unclean. Indeed, I suspect that there are now a few who regard the famous Barmendi as an enlightened food reformer, vastly in advance of his age. Sancho had to leave to eat wafers and conserve of quinces; the Barmendi guest had nothing at all.

One of the queerest incidences of this system of medicine has just fallen into my hands. It is a pamphlet of 1850, and it is called "The Homeopathic Cure of Toothache by Smelling." But the smelling of certain drugs and medicaments is the lightest part of the treatment. Its backbone is the list of things that you must not eat or drink. You must not dream of coffee, tea, spirituous or fermented liquors, vinegar, lemons. You must forbear all that is pungent, such as mustard, horseradish, and herrings. No spices must be tasted, honey and syrup must be laid aside. Onions, celery, garlic, sorrel, asparagus, mushrooms, new or stale white bread, geese, ducks, salmon, oysters are forbidden. Tobacco in any form is poison; so also are all strong and aromatic odours. All mustard plasters must be avoided; also all bathing.

There is a thoroughness about this follower of Doctor Pedro Recio.

It is claimed, I see, that the "Vanity Bag" is a German invention, dating from 1881. But, surely, there were Vanity Bags long before. What about the "women's ridicules" that Mr. Noah Claypole proposed to empty? Indeed, I seem to remember medieval brasses on which noble ladies carried what must have been Vanity Bags—"gypciéres"—save that the handle was much longer than in the modern mode.

A singular point struck me in the matter of the small Egyptian idol that brings bad luck, to which "Observator" called attention in last week's *Observer*. It is this: No belief in omens, arms, periapts, talismans, mascots, or any such fooleries. I never touch wood, I never throw spilled salt over my shoulder, I never go out of my way to avoid walking under a ladder. Yet I would not have that Egyptian idol as a gift.

Some years ago I was of a party that was being conducted around the British Museum. In the mummy room the guide pointed to a particular case, saying, "That is the case which is supposed to bring disaster on anyone who goes near it. You can go look at it if you like." We were in a huddle on the other side of the room. We stayed on the other side of the room; every man jack of us. Yet I knew perfectly well that the mummy legend, like many other legends of a like kind, was an entirely modern invention: I think it has been ascribed to the late W. T. Stead. I knew all this, just as I know that the Egyptian idol cannot have any kind of influence, good or bad, on my life or anyone else's life. And yet, what do we know? After all, it is impossible to prove the impotence for evil of the idol or of the mummy. So why take the risk of possessing the one or of approaching the other? So infinite, so subtle, are the grades of belief and unbelief.

The English doctor—he was Akenside in caricature—who gave the Banquet after the Manner of the Ancients in "Peregrine Pickle," was a good deal mortified because he had to flavour the soup with assafetida instead of the nitron of the ancients. But he needs not have been distressed. His substituted ingredient was a well-known relish in the old world, if the grammarians are right and identifying silphium as assafetida. The British Museum has acquired a coin of Cyrene, bearing on its obverse the effigy of this silphium plant, which made the prosperity of the country. Aristophanes commends it when mashed up with cheese; a sort of Cyrenaic Rabbit.

Well, you can get assafetida at any chemists; but I think I will apply the Logic of the Idol and the Mummy—and take no risks.

A few weeks ago I was speaking of the ancient City Guild of the Fellowship Porters; of their old, half-forgotten splendours when they went once a year to one of the City churches to hear a service, bearing nosegays in their hands, of their feasts when the silver bowls shown on the board, of the mysterious grades in the brotherhood, by which the carryer of fruit was set apart from the mere coal porter. The little note brought me a sad letter from Mr. W. C. Murphy, of 102 Stamford-street, Blackfriars; "Fellowship Porter and Freeman of the City of London" as he subscribes himself.

It seems that since the Company was dissolved more than thirty years ago, the world has not been too kind to the survivors. There are about thirty of the Fellowship still alive. Their average age is 74; and they would be glad of "even a few shillings a week or a month." Well; it is not for me, who have no franchise in the Liberty of the City to advise Masters and Wardens and Courts of Assistance; but would it not be well if the wealthy remaining Guilds took some thought to the old perished Fellowship and its surviving brethren? To another class I can appeal more confidently since to this brotherhood I belong. Let all of us who have tasted Miss Abbey Potterson's Early Purl, who have partaken of her Flip, and relished her Burnt Sherry do our best to see that the old boys are Thirty Jolly Fellowship Porters for the rest of their days.

Thirty

October 31, 1926

Character, I think, is all-important in evidence. There are people one knows whose simplest statement is received with a certain hesitation and reserve. Smith, for example, may say that he met Jones in the Strand, and you will likely reflect that it *may* possibly be so. Likely enough, Smith is not a deliberate liar, but merely hopelessly loose-minded and inaccurate; at all events his every word is received with a tincture of doubt. With Robinson, on the other hand, the case is very different. If he declared that he saw Jones levitated in Pall Mall, you would give the matter your most serious and respected attention.

Well, Robinson—as we will call him—was telling me the other day an odd experience that had once befallen him. Robinson, it should be said, is an actor, and an old Bensonian. And in his Bensonian time, he dreamed one night that he was obliged to take up a new part at a very brief notice. In his dream, he found himself in the wings, nervous about his text, and not too clear as to his entrances, his exits, and the general business of the scenes in which he was engaged. His only comfort was that Arthur Whitby—then and for many years a member of the Benson company—stood beside him in the wings and coached him in the business of the part as the play proceeded. But at a certain queue, this abettor and comforter seemed to be withdrawn. Robinson rushed on and found himself, in his own phrase, "ballooning into Mrs. Benson." He had entered on a word-cue; he had not been instructed that Mrs. Benson had certain business alone on the stage, for which the actor had to delay his entrance.

The next morning Robinson went down to rehearsal. The play for the night was "Macbeth"; and Robinson was told at once that Mr. Whitby had lost his voice: could he play Banquo? He did so, and, as in the dream, Whitby stood by him in the wings, seeing him through the part. And, as in the dream, he failed to receive the necessary caution as to the delayed entrance, made a premature appearance, and so interfered to a certain extent with Lady Macbeth's business. And as I have known Robinson for nearly a quarter of a century, and know him to be a truth-telling and accurate man, I believe every word of this odd story.

And the point of it is, be it noted, that there is no point. *Neu deus intersit*: And in this case the *nodus* was by no means important enough to justify the intervention of a prophetic dream. And, further, the dream warning had no effect: the small catastrophe happened in spite of it. This is usually the case in this queer world of "warnings." It was so in the case of a well-known officer, who had a presentiment that he would lose his right hand; so strong a presentiment, indeed, that he taught himself to write with his left hand. The war came and the officer lost his right foot.

At the bicentenary celebrations of St. Martin-in-the-Fields, the Bishop of Willesden spoke of the eighteenth century church atmosphere in which "enthusiasm was considered a vice." So it was alleged that the famous imposter Elizabeth Canning was an enthusiast, and had been tutored and buoyed up by the Methodists. But the charge of enthusiasm was refuted by the Rector of Saint Mary Magdalen, Old Fish-street, who had ministered to Elizabeth in Newgate. He declared that so far from the girl showing any signs of enthusiasm, she professed herself a member of the Church of England.

This is not quite so funny as it sounds. The enthusiasm of the eighteenth century implied religious hysteria, with external manifestations of the convulsive order. The "enthusiasts" would interrupt the proceedings of the meeting with loud cries proclaiming their assurance of salvation; they might foam at the mouth, they occasionally fell down in fits. All this would seem mighty offensive to a Churchman such as Johnson, though he was an ardent religious enthusiast, using the word in its modern sense.

Old bills are always interesting. There are some curious notes of expenses in the very pleasant "Cruise Upon Wheels," by Charles Collins, Dickens's son-in-law, which Mr. Peter Davies has wisely reprinted. The two travellers of the book drove themselves from Calais to Switzerland, and seem to have been much impressed by "the extraordinary cheapness of the French inns." Well, considering that the date of the tour was 1860, and that most of the towns visited were off the main track, small, and unvisited by tourists, I hardly think that there was anything extraordinary in the cheapness of the hotel bills. Thus, at St. Pol, Hotel d'Angleterre, for supper, lodging, breakfast, and horse's keep, the charge was 17s. 11d. At Sens, dinner, three nights lodging, two entire days, and horse's keep, cost £2 19s. 7d.; and the Champagnole bill for dinner, beds, breakfast, and horse's keep, was £13s. 9d. Champagnole is a large village, the inn was "not bad," though the fowl was very tough, and had evidently been hurried straight from the slaughter to the spit. If we allow the horse the odd three-and-ninepence, I cannot think that the two travellers paid very cheaply for the accommodation they describe.

The Paris correspondent of *The Observer*, describing the singular prehistoric "finds" near Vichy, makes an extremely significant point in noting that amongst the Neolithic objects discovered—dating from about 4,000 B. C.—there were certain things made after a distinctly paleolithic pattern. Hence, it may be concluded, the gulf between the old and new Stone Ages was nothing like so vast as has been contended. The paleolithic tradition had survived; and, very likely, I would surmise, the paleolithic man.

Thirty-one

November 7, 1926

"Electricity is the life-blood of the universe, but its own nature is an unsolved mystery." Thus Professor Andrade, who speaks with full authority; and I cannot help feeling certain scruples. As rational beings above all, have we any real right to have anything to do with unsolved mysteries? Should I be writing these lines by the light of an electric lamp? Ought we to use the Tube railways or the Underground? What is to be said in defense of "wiring" and electric heating apparatus?

For, as I say, we are rational beings. We have been taught, again and again, to deride all doctrines and all practices which cannot be explained, which elude the tests of sturdy common sense, which remain unsolved mysteries. Churches and realms have been turned upside down because they depended on mysterious doctrines incapable of logical explanation. And yet we send telegrams to one another without scruple, and do not always refuse to travel by electrified railways.

Perhaps it is as well. No man hath seen a vitamin at any time; and probably, if we are determined to be purely and absolutely rational in all things we should speedily cease to exist. For in a world of uncertainty this one thing is absolutely certain: that we have no real knowledge of any material thing whatsoever. The only real knowledge is of spiritual things, and that is in the possession of the saints, the poets, and the painters.

Bishop Berkeley wrote a singular work called "Siris." It began by praising the virtues of a medical preparation, Tar Water, prepared, if I remember, by allowing a certain quantity of water to stand on tar. The practice seems simple enough, and the treatise begins simply by showing that tar contains in a very special manner the heat and energy and life-giving force of the sun, from which it proceeds. But from this plain beginning "Siris" soars into the Empyrean and beyond it, into heights far beyond me.

I do not know how Tar Water succeeded as a practical remedy. It was revived in the nineteenth century, and certain hints as to its exhibition and effects may be found in a treatise called "Great Expectations." "Some medical beast," says Pip, "had revived Tar Water in these days as a fine medicine, and Mrs. Joe always kept a supply of it in the cupboard; having a belief in its virtues correspondent to its nastiness."

And then, it will be remembered, Pip, stealing brandy for the convict, inadvertently filled the bottle with Tar Water, and Mr. Pumblechook, partaking of the said brandy, made a most dreadful fuss, and Pip adds significantly: "I knew he would be worse by-and-by." On the whole, one does not get a very good impression of the famous remedy. Perhaps Bishop Berkeley's idea has been fulfilled more happily in the aspirins— also a tar preparation—which Sir Thomas Horder has just been praising so highly.

I was noting the other day that, in the Celtic tradition at all events, the fairies are rather beings of ill will than of good. It is hard to find any link between them and the gracious following of Oberon and Titania. And I have just lit on a curious confirmation of their ill character in Miss Somerville's "Wheel-Tracks." Miss Somerville relates how her brother and herself were reading "Alice in Wonderland" one sunny morning in the 'sixties. The two children were in their grandmother's sitting room. "It was high summer, and the three windows of the room were wide open; from one of them one can see out over the harbour to the open sea, the two others look on the croquet ground and towards the avenue. Suddenly, we heard from, as it seemed, the avenue, a rushing outbreak of music, richer and more delicious—as I remember it—than any music that I have heard before or since."

The children thought it was a German band playing, and rushed out to ask for more. But there was no band to be seen and nobody but themselves had heard any music at all, and they were pooh-poohed and derided.

There is no hint of evil here. That follows in the case of one Thade MacSweeny, sailor, who, going down to the quay one night very late, "saw a girl coming up the hill to him." ... Thade thought it was too late for her to be out, and he said it to her. She made him no answer, and he grabbed at the shawl she had on her, and it was like nothing, and there was no one there." And then "the lane was filled with music," and Thade ran down the hill, terrified, to the little house on the quay. "And 'tis a good thing for you that the house was here before you," said the man who pulled him safe indoors. "It's a bad job for them that that music follows."

Miss Somerville says that she never heard the fairy music again; but that her sister has heard it twice, the second time in December, 1922. And I think we may compare with these experiences the very serious and straightforward account of the naval officer who was on duty on the morning when the German Navy came in and surrendered. All the while he and many others heard the steady beating of a drum, it being quite out of the question that any actual drum should be beaten on board that ship or any other ship.

This strange experience was connected with the legendary "Drake's Drum"; but when we try to account for these wonders we begin to go astray. I think we may safely say that certain people experience sensations of sight, sound, and odour which are not of the natural—or rather, usual—order. But having admitted the fact, it is well to leave it as an unsolved mystery—like electricity.

Of course there is the temptation to declare all these occult experiences to be purely subjective hallucinations, to be classed with the rats and snakes of delirium tremens. This theory may pass when there is only one percipient; but if there be more than one, as in Miss Somerville's story, and in the case of "Drake's Drum"? When people were exciting themselves unnecessarily about certain dubious "Angels of Mons," a distinguished calvary officer wrote to me concerning a remarkable experience that had befallen him during the famous retreat. Not only he, but many of his brother officers, and many of his men were sure they were accompanied by calvary moving parallel with them at a little distance off. A reconnoitering party was sent out, and found nothing. But what had happened?

Thirty-two

November 14, 1926

In "In Black and White," Lord Knutsford's book of recollections, there is a notable instance of will-power. Lord Knutsford heard detail from the late Lord Kitchener. "If the sahib will not grant me this," said a native of India to Kitchener, "I will die at his door-step." The request was not granted, and the Indian went out and fell dead in the doorway.

The authority is good, and we may safely credit the story. But what a pity it is that this will-power, or imagination-power seems always, or nearly always, to work on what may be called the dark side. We have the phrase "frightened to death," but we have no such phrase as "exalted to life." There is, indeed, a story of an aged lady of quality—I can give no names—who was told that her choice lay between an operation and speedy death. She is reported to have answered "I won't have an operation, and I won't die," and to have lived for many happy and healthy years afterwards. But I am not sure that the tale is veracious, and, anyhow such cases are very rare. We can easily be persuaded that we are miserably ill: who will persuade us that we are triumphantly well?

It is some weeks since I was saying how much I should welcome news from Spain of a domestic rather than a high political type. I think I wanted to know what the Curate had for dinner, whether the Barber had turned into a country doctor, and how the gentry, the hidalgos and caballeros, furnished their drawing-rooms. Well, here is an item of homely interest, though, to be sure, the tiresome political element enters into it. It is announced that a farm at Argamasilla, owned by General Aguilera, has been sold by auction, to recover a fine of £6,600 for political plotting, imposed on him by General Primo de Rivera. I care nothing about the plots, the plotters, or the counterplotters, but I think we may conclude that agriculture is in a tolerably prosperous condition at Argamasilla, and we must be glad, for it is agreed that Argamasilla de Alba, is the "patria feliz del hidalgo caballero Don Quixote de la Mancha," that "village of La Mancha, the name of which I have no desire to recollect."

When mayor succeeds mayor at Grantham, it seems that the retiring mayor's robe is stripped from him, while the town clerk taps his head with a mallet, signifying that all is over. There is a singular custom obtaining in one of the City companies at the election of a new Master. The retiring Master, the wardens, and the assistants being met, a hat is produced and handed to the Master. He tries to put it on, and finds that it will not fit; others make the experiment with a like result. Finally, the Master Designate takes the hat, it fits perfectly, and the new Master's year of office begins—the hat, of course, having been carefully made to his measure. We may also compare the curious initiatory ceremony of the French butchers, as described in "Le Moyen de Parvenir" (c. 1610). The candidate was first stripped of all his clothes. He was then directed to put them on again. This done; he was acclaimed by the assembled brethren "You are now a Master Butcher; you have dressed a calf." Many of us will recall other ceremonies of a more secret nature; not that it is suggested that the latter are in any sense derived from the former, rather that both proceed from the same soil, and were probably invented in or about the same period.

Dr. Harry Campbell, who has been lecturing lately on that perpetually interesting subject, eating and drinking, says that man's simian ancestor grew his wits and became a man by giving up vegetables and taking to hunting, with the result of hunting, meat. "It was noteworthy," said the lecturer, "that man evolved from a speechless being to a being capable of abstract thought—almost, indeed, to his present status without cultivated grain, any other milk than his mother's, eggs, sugar, alcohol, tea, or coffee. He could still survive and thrive without any of these things."

And so, I supposed, the conclusion would be that he should go back to a diet composed almost exclusively of meat, with an occasional root and a nut or two now and then as a relish. But, oddly enough, the diet recommended by Dr. Campbell to modern man consists of crusty bread and butter, raw fruit, and salad. But we have seen that the monkey grew into a man by leaving off vegetables and taking to meat. Bread and butter were unknown to him. There seems to be a gap between the doctor's premises and his conclusion.

Dr. Campbell's courage, I suspect, failed him. He was addressing Food Reformers, and shrank from praising chops and steaks. I disagree heartily, both from premise and conclusion. I do not think that a diet of bread and butter, fruit, and lettuces would be in the least amusing; and it must be remembered that no food, whether bodily or ghostly, which fails to amuse and interest can be of the least use or benefit to any man. If I read "Lycidas" and enjoy it not, it profits nothing; if I eat lettuce and enjoy it not, it profits nothing. And, on the other hand, the remarks about the diet of primitive man involve by implication the old fallacy of the return to nature, that is, to savagery. There is a colony near Grasse which is busily engaged in returning to nature. There are no laws or police; human relations depend entirely upon free-will and natural instincts. Marriage is not recognised, and children are brought up by the community. The children are naked, the grown-ups almost naked—and the neighbours complained to the police. And the odd thing is that the foolish people who mimic savages do it so badly. True savagery is stuffed with rules and regulations, and marriage laws of the Australian Blackfellows are extremely complex.

Thirty-three

November 21, 1926

Strange things have been written recently by Mr. R. M. MacDonald, a prospector, concerning the pygmies of New Guinea. These little people are about 42 in. high, steadily built, and almost covered with light gray hair. They have voices like megaphones, can blow tiny darts through tubes with an unerring precision, and carry those needle-like missiles in their frizzed hair.

The oddest thing about them is that they hold in strict subjection certain tribes of giant cannibals, who live about them and defend them against all outsiders. The giants are fierce and mighty against all white men—they have never been brought under foreign rule—but they are the humble servants of the dwarfs, whom they regard as magicians. Cf.—as the scholars say—the case of old Maunders, who had in his cottage in Spa Fields in the winter-time when the season was over, "eight male and female dwarfs sitting down to dinner every day, who was waited on by eight old giants in green coats, red smalls, blue cotton stockings, and high-lows; and there was one dwarf as had grown elderly and wicious, who whenever his giant wasn't quick enough to please him used to stick pins in his legs." The principle of the matter evidently remains the same in Spa Fields as in New Guinea. But in the latter piece, the dwarfs seem to be born "wicious." And note, by the way, word "high-lows." We call them boots, but a hundred years ago boots came up to the knee, as they still do in America. There, if I remember, our boots are known as "Oxfords."

Another point about these entertaining pygmies of New Guinea. They say that "about midway through time" their ancestors, who were bird-men, were compelled by a great flood to fly to the mountains where the dwarfs now live. And is there any country on earth where there is no tradition of a great flood? I think the learned and ingenious author of "The Golden Bough" holds that all the flood traditions are vastly exaggerated recollections of local river floods. This theory is hardly satisfactory, but I suppose it would never do to hold that mankind at large remembered the end of the Glacial period and a melting of the whole world of ice.

A week or two ago we were talking about the fatal mummy case of the British Museum, which brings death, and a certain idol which involves the possessor in disaster. I remarked that I had not the faintest belief in the malefic power of either; but for all that, took care to keep out of the way of both. After all, the universe is a mystery; we cannot be quite sure of anything; so why take a needless risk? It would not be fair, I think, to ascribe this obscure shadow of the belief to the Musgraves of Edenhall. It is true that their fairy goblet—now on view for a few weeks at the Victoria and Albert Museum—the Luck of Edenhall, has been preserved in its ancient leather case in the Bank of England for many years; but it does not follow that the Musgraves get even the faintest shadow of credence to the couplet:—

If e'er that cup should break or fall,
Farewell the Luck of Edenhall.

The diction of the prophecy strikes me as suspiciously modern, but the glass itself is undoubtedly ancient and has been an heirloom for many centuries. One understands that an ancient family would grieve if such a possession were shattered, all questions of luck, good or bad, apart. But the luck of Edenhall belongs to a very interesting group of objects: the talismans or palladia. It is probable that the Coronation Stone, which we stole from the Scots, was once such an object; and I suppose that if it were missing from Westminster Abbey we should be seriously annoyed, though few would fear that the fortune of Britain was over. And I have no doubt that the Holy Grail was, to a certain extent, the baptised descendant of a British talisman, on which the prosperity first of a particular tribe, and then the whole race, depended. Scott derived the talisman with which Saladin healed King Richard from an object in the possession of a Scottish family—called, if I remember, the Lucky Penny. I think I must have heard the end of this old song. An aunt of mine told me that when she was a girl at Builth (c.1815) a family in the neighbourhood once owned a magic stone, which was lent to people whose cattle were ailing. The stone was placed in a vessel of water, and the water given to the sick beasts. It will be noted that the Talisman had become veterinary in its use: it was no longer applied to the ills of humanity.

Many of the Southwark Councillors are indignant with the Priest-Vicar of the Cathedral, the Rev. C. B. Roach, for telling the truth about the slums of the Borough; but one of them is confused as well. This Councillor is reported to have said that if the preacher's remarks had been made by a member of the congregation, "he would have been brought before a magistrate for brawling." The Councillor does not understand the matter of the offence. He and his friends who protested aloud during the delivery of the sermon were brawlers, and the one Councillor who interjected "Hear, hear!" was also a brawler. Any utterance from the congregation not set down or provided for—as in forbidding of banns—in the Book of Common Prayer constitutes brawling. It is a question whether all hymns, excepting the "Veni Creator" in the Ordinal, and doubtfully accepting the anthem in quires and places where they sing, are not brawlings set to music.

Thirty-four

November 28, 1926

In 1822 King George IV. paid a visit of state to Edinburgh. Sir Walter Scott was the virtual Master of the Ceremonies, and Sir Walter made these ceremonies a Pageant of the Highlands. Lockhart was amazed and a little scandalised. As he remarks: "With all respect and admiration for the noble and generous qualities which our countrymen of the Highland Clans have so often exhibited, it was difficult to forget that they had always constituted a small and almost always an unimportant part of the Scottish population." And so again, when the magistrates of Edinburgh entertained their Sovereign at a banquet, the King proposed the one toast of "The Chieftains and Clans of Scotland— and prosperity to the land of Cakes." Scott, as Lockhart notes, had hallucinated himself into the belief that to all intents and purposes the Scots were Highland Celts; and he communicated this hallucination to George IV. It is almost as if the King, visiting Norwich, were to drink to the immortal memory of Cadwaladyr Vendigeid and Owen Glencwr, as representative East Anglians.

And the hallucination has endured. There is to be a Scots dinner at the Savoy on St. Andrew's Day, and a Dictionary is to be provided, "for the benefit of those Sassenachs who, ignorant of the Scottish language and its poetry, may find it difficult to make themselves understood." The words and phrases in question are from Lowland Scots, which is as Sassenach a dialect as that of Dorset or Devon. Burns did not write in Gaelic any more than Barnes wrote in Welsh.

The writer of the delightful article on the New Forest in last week's *Observer*, enumerating some of the place-names of "The Magic Wood," asks his readers where they suppose the New Foresters got such a name as Rhinefield Walk. Well, I conjecture that adjacent to this walk there is, or once was, a waterway. The water-filled ditches that intersect the level lands of North Somerset are called rheens, and I suppose with hesitation, since etymology is a perilous science, that rheen and Rhine and Rhone and Rhondda are variants of a word that meant a water course a long time ago. River names endure.

There is a demonstration in the pure science of Geometry called the *reductio ad absurdum*. The secret of this procedure seems to have been lost in the mixed sciences. A distinguished physician has just said that "all the clothes actually necessary in good health are a loin-cloth and warm boots." And I am inclined to think that it was this same physician who declared four or five years ago that Mr. Squeers's system of "grazing"—the sending of delicate boys into carrot and turnip fields to eat as many raw roots as they liked—constituted an ideal diet. Let us imagine the "scientific" dinner-party; the ladies and gentlemen in loin-cloths and warm boots eating many sorts of raw roots. That is the *reductio ad absurdum*. The premises which laid to so monstrous a conclusion may safely be neglected; since they are assuredly false.

I was saying the other day that while we have the phrase "frightened to death," we, unfortunately, have no such phrase as "exalted to life." And, it seems, we not only have the phrase "frightened to death," but the grim reality. Almost three weeks ago two boys, both named Gray, but not related to one another, went for an afternoon's lark in the woods near Lebanon, New Hampshire. Fred had a toy revolver, and a bough caught the hammer and exploded the cartridge. The other boy Roland Gray, "dropped in his tracks," and Fred, making sure that he had killed his friend, rushed away and drowned himself. Then, Roland's parents, hearing of this, and knowing that their son had been with Fred, searched the woods. Roland was found dead, and the bullet dropped from the clothes. It had made a tiny bruise on the skin over the heart. The boy had died of fright, and his conviction that a bullet striking the body near the heart was mortal.

There is another example of fright recorded in last week's papers, which, I hope, will have no such sad results. A Westmoreland school teacher, girl of twenty-five, was preparing for a certificate examination. Among the subjects proposed for the examination was, oddly enough, Wilkie Collins's "Woman in White"; and, more oddly, the poor girl told her sister that the book was frightening her so much that she was afraid to read any more. So the kind sister furnished an oral précis of the dread machinations of the Count Fosco; whereupon the examinand disappeared! The story has its sad side—there is always a sad side to these affairs of certificates and examinations—but one fears that the ghost of Wilkie Collins must be gratified.

Thirty-five

December 5, 1926

"Instinct" is one of the most convenient words in the language. We say that birds and cats and dogs and bees do this, that, and the other "by instinct," and the phrase is accepted as quite comfortable and satisfactory; as a lucid and rational explanation of the doings of the creatures aforesaid. We feel that our understanding of the matter is clear and complete.

But, as a matter of hard fact, when we say that a dog or an elephant does so-and-so by instinct, we really mean that it acts as it does by and through a power which, for us, is utterly mysterious, occult, and unknowable. The animal consciousness, animal process of action, glibly ascribed to instinct, constitute for us a hidden and unsearchable world; all the more mysterious in as much as many animals possess, in addition, considerable powers of reasoning. I believe the tale of the dog who was cured at a hospital, and sometime afterwards took a wounded fellow to the hospital door, is veridical: and here, I would say, you have reason of pretty much the same quality as reason in men. But what about the story that Sir Wilfrid Lawson, Master of the Cumberland Foxhounds, told the other day at Carlisle? A pack of hounds was sent to Cumberland by train. On the first occasion of their being taken out hunting, disappeared. Eventually—the period is not specified in the report before me—they reappeared at their old kennels in Sussex.

And how on earth did they do it? The distance between the Sussex and the Cumberland kennels is, let us say, 350 miles. The hounds were conveyed in a closed van and shunted, I suppose, round London from the southern to the northern line, after the fashion of touring actors. The beasts had no opportunities of viewing the scenery or of taking marks of the country through which they went. Furthermore, it is pretty certain that they did not return to Sussex by the permanent way, or even by the high road. They went, no doubt, across country, and if they were seen by anyone, were taken for strays from the local pack. And, again: how did these hounds find their way through 350 miles of unknown territory? To me, at all events, this is a question without an answer. The one faculty of the foxhound is its scent; but I cannot think that the hounds could scent the Sussex kennels in far-off Cumberland.

The story of the rooks, told on the authority of that expert in country things, "P. W. D. I.," of the "Daily Mail," is, really, as mysterious, though not so startling on the surface. This is a case of rooks who were accustomed to build, year by year, in a certain elm tree near a house. One spring, instead of setting about the repair of the old nests as usual, the birds held a two-days' council in the tree—and then they demolished the nests and flew away to look for new quarters. Five months later the baby of the house attached to the old rookery, who was born during the destruction of the nests, was being taken out in the perambulator and passed under the condemned tree. It was a perfectly calm day; but, without warning, one of the branches crashed to the ground, missing nurse and baby by a few inches. When the branch was down the flaw was clearly seen. Are we, then, to suppose rooks dowered with an innate faculty of detecting unsound boughs? If so, why the two days' council, which would seem to imply various opinions, the discussion of pros and cons, and a reasoned argument leading to a logical conclusion? One knows not which of the two explanations is the more preposterous.

Mr. G. B. Besant's "City Churches and Their Memories," full of pleasantly-conveyed learning, appears most appropriately as if to celebrate the crowning mercy of the decision of the House of Commons. I confess that this decision and the size of the majority in its favour were to me as much of a surprise as a delight. The futilitarian point of views is generally victorious in these days. I once met a man who maintained that cathedrals were a scandalous waste of money. He said that iron churches would have done just as well, and the money saved might have been given to the poor. He turned out to be a traveller in the iron industry. I do not think that he was aware that he had very ancient authority for his remark about the poor.

It was only last week that we were talking about the strange fantasies of science, when it applies itself to diet; and now an unfortunate man has perished through taking the dietetic writers seriously. Poor Colonel Call breakfasted on an orange and three grapes, and dined on a potato, half a lettuce, a teaspoonful of raw scraped carrot, a teaspoonful of raw scraped beetroot, two dry biscuits, and a little butter. It is odd to think that this sad regimen is just the sort of diet that commended itself to Shelley. He is described by Haydon (who has recently been reprinted) as making a ghastly meal of a cauliflower, while he spoke hard things in a gentle voice against the Christian religion. And Mr. Bumble must be quoted on the same side. When confronted with the wickedness of Oliver Twist, he declared, it will be remembered, that the boy's violence was caused, not by madness, but by Meat.

Thirty-six

December 12, 1926

White's Club, I see, has reorganised its proprietorship and has become a private company. It is curious that, while we can date the foundation of White's Chocolate House pretty accurately—1698 is generally accepted—it is difficult to say exactly when and how the public chocolate house became the private club. The matter was not clear to the writers of the eighteenth century, as it appears from the "Life of Garrick," by Davies; that Davies who kept the bookseller's shop in Russell-street, Covent Garden, and introduced Boswell to Johnson. Davies is speaking of Colley Cibber:—

"Colley, we are told, had the honour to be a member of the great club at Whites; and so, I suppose, might any man who wore good clothes and paid his money when he lost it."

Such a club would not be a club at all. And yet, when Mr. Arthur, proprietor, was "burnt out of White's Chocolate House in 1733," he announces that he has moved to Gaunt's Coffee House, where he humbly begs "all noblemen and gentlemen" to favour him with their company as usual. And, yet again, there is a list of members and a book of rules of "the old Club at White's," dated 1736, only three years after the fire.

I should think that the solution of the puzzle is to be found in the phrase "the old Club at White's." Originally, White's was a public chocolate house, open to any man who was decently dressed. In the natural course of things, a particular set of men took to frequenting it, while another set of men were to be found at White's, and yet another set frequented the Grecian. You may observe the like state of affairs to this day at Little Pedlington: The customer of the Green Dragon is but rarely seen at the Mitre, and the King's Head people are to be found, night by night, at the King's Head. But in the case of White's, as I conjecture, an inner circle was formed from the general concourse of customers. At first, perhaps, this inner circle had a certain corner of the public room reserved for its peculiar use; then a private room was set apart for the members, and finally, the "Club at White's" overflowed its bounds, took possession of the whole house, and so became "White's." The process was, no doubt, a gradual one; an early stage is described in "Defoe's Journey Through England":—

"I must not forget to tell you that the parties have their different places, where, however, a stranger is always well received; but a Whig will no more go to the Cocoa-Tree or Ozinda's than a Tory will be seen at the Coffee House of St. James's."

"Basto, ma'am; you have spadille, I believe." Does anybody still play quadrille—I think that is the name —after the fashion of those dear Cranford ladies? I should not be surprised. A few days ago I was looking at an advertisement of Christmas gifts, reflecting, perhaps a little sadly, that neither the barking monkey nor the model locomotive would do me very much good in these late days, when my eye was caught by the Mahogany Games Compendium. There were chess, draughts, and dominoes, naturally enough; yet then came cribbage, which I had thought of either as extinct, or else lingering in very dim back parlours of dim old country towns. After this, it was no longer amazing to find that bézique, but it was fifty-five years ago, and I once joined an old gentleman who was born in the eighteenth century, and might well have been one of Mr. Wardie's guests at Dingley Dell. I remember that he liked the game to go "with a great haloo." He was evidently in the veritable tradition of the game; when Mr. Wardie presided at the Pope John board he was "in the very height of his jollity; and he was so funny in his management of the board, and the ladies were so sharp after their winnings, that the whole table was in a perpetual roar of merriment and laughter." But, to tell the truth, I had thought these old games all dead and forgotten together. Evidently not, and so much the better. For anything I know, all fours, the favoured game of Dr. Haggage of the Marshalsea, has its lovers.

Sometime ago, speaking of the Luck of Eden Hall, and other talismans and wonder-objects, I mentioned a certain marvellous stone kept at Builth, the particulars of which I heard long ago from an old aunt of mine. The recollections of old age will sometimes falter, and I have been handsomely set right in the matter by Mr. Roger Williams, of Builth Wells, a local antiquary.

"The Magic Stone of which you write," he says, "was undoubtedly the stone that was famous in Central Wales up to about seventy years ago as a cure for the bites of mad dogs. The origin of the stone is unknown, but tradition has it that one hot summer's day, when mad dogs were numerous, it dropped from heaven as the Gift of God to man. It was placed in the custody of the Thomas's of Welfield, or, as it is now called, Cefndyris, near Builth Wells. The general belief about the stone some sixty years ago was, that in spite of the fact that a large quantity of scrapings was taken from the stone every year, it neither diminished in size nor weight. To cure a person bitten by a mad dog, sufficient scrapings from the stone to cover a threepenny piece were required, and this scraping or stone dust was placed in milk, and had to be drunk by the person affected."

This Magic Stone is, I am glad to say, still in the possession of the Hereditary Keepers. Its relief is no longer sought out by the afflicted, since, owing to the operations of the Board of Agriculture, there are no mad dogs left: An odd ending to a very old tale. But to those interested in Grail origins, I would point out the phrase, "it dropped from heaven, as the Gift of God to man." St. David received a "hallowed altar," which was called "the Gift from Heaven." St. Carannoc possessed "an honourable altar from on high." The Grail in the Parsifal is a stone called Lapsit Exillit, or, as I suggest, *Lapis ex coelis*, the Stone from Heaven. The great thing and the small thing both grew out of the same soil.

Arthur Machen

Thirty-seven [1]

December 19, 1926

We were puzzling our heads the other day about the pack of hounds which, kenneled in Cumberland, found their way back across country to their original quarters in Sussex. And here is another hound problem, still more perplexing. I gather it from a correspondent, a member of an Irish family which migrated from Ireland in the early 'eighties—when the land league flourished—because the agrarian troubles had made fox-hunting impossible.

These Irish people settled down with their horses in North Devon, and joined the Exmoor Hunt. The head of the house sent over to Queen's County for two or three couple of foxhounds to augment the Exmoor pack. "The first day," my correspondent writes, "they went out, two of the hounds were missing in the afternoon. Three days later they were found near the Seacoast in Pembrokeshire, having got thus far on their way home to Ireland. As they could not get to Milford Haven by the way they came, which had been by train to Swansea and then steamer, these hounds had travelled way up the Devon and Somerset side of the Severn until they found means to cross it and then down the Welsh side."

The course which they actually took implies a knowledge of the geography of the British Isles, absurd, and more than absurd. For, it will be noted, their journey from Devonshire to some point between Newport and Gloucester was dead against their sense of direction, supposing such a sense to exist. Their Irish home lay to the north-west; they ran up past Bristol to the north-east. Can we suppose that one hound observed to the other: "This, you see, is the Bristol Channel. It narrows considerably, and eventually becomes the Severn. If we follow the coast in a north-easterly direction we shall be able to cross the river and run down through Gloucestershire, Monmouthshire, Glanmorganshire, Carmarthenshire, Pembrokeshire, till we get to Milford Haven. There, we shall have no difficulty in finding a boat to take us back to the Ould Counthry"? To me it is utterly incredible that such a process should take place in the mind of a foxhound. But how did the two hounds get to Milford Haven?

---

1 Due to the poor state of the source material, this installment has been truncated.

...

The Kit-Kat club, which was subject to a visitation—we will not say a raid—by the police a week ago, is not a successor, save in name, to the famous club of Queen Anne's days. At the modern Kit-Kat, they dance, at the ancient one, which met in Shire-lane, thirty distinguished noblemen and gentlemen, zealots for the House of Hanover and the Protestant succession, took counsel together against the exiled House of Stuart: "the people that saved Britain," Horace Walpole writes of them.

We saw last week that the later eighteenth century had very vague notions as to the origin of White's Club: but the men who were contemporaries of the past members of the Kit-Kat Club were even more undecided as to the derivation of the name. Defoe said that the club was so-called because it first met "at the house of one Christopher Catt." The "Spectator" thought that Kit-Kat was an old name for a mutton-pie, and one is reminded of the ingenious young man, vender of pies, known to Mr. Samuel Weller.

"'They're all made o'them noble animals,' says he, a pointin' to a wery nice little tabby kitten, 'and I seasons 'em for beefsteak, weal, or kidney, 'cordin' to the demand. And more than that,' says he, 'I can make a weal a beefsteak, or a beefsteak a kidney, or any one of 'em a mutton, at a minute notice.'"

Another contemporary, Ned Ward ("The London Spy") says that the title derived from a man named Christopher, who kept a house of entertainment at the sign of the Cat and Fiddle, and Malone, writing seventy or eighty years later, adopting the Christopher Catt hypothesis, thinks that this man gave his name to the pies, as the Earl of Sandwich godfathered the sandwich, and that the pies gave their name to the thirty Protestant noblemen and gentlemen who devoured them. The surmise of the poet, that the club got its name from its habit of toasting young Kits and old Cats, maybe dismissed as frivolous.

Caerleon-on-Usk slept a long sleep of fifteen hundred years or so: and suddenly it has once more become illustrious. Scarcely a week passes without its name appearing in the papers, and I am sure that its citizens—I am happy to boast myself one of them—should exult. But I cannot think that Mr. Charles B. Cochran's proposal with respect to my native place is all together practical. The distinguished producer asks, in the "Daily Mail," "Why not plays again at Caerleon?"—that is in the Roman Amphitheatre, called King Arthur's Round Table. Well, in the first place there never were any plays given there. The amphitheatre or circus was used for wild beast baiting and for gladiatorial fights; plays were produced in a theatre, a building of quite a different structure, with a raised stage. In fact, a circus was a circus, and a playhouse a playhouse in Roman days as in our days; and, to the best of my recollection, the little Amphitheatre at Caerleon is just about the size of the modern circus ring. And, then, Mr. Cochran talks of reviving chariot races. Alas! the Caerleon structure is much too small for that. There is no room there for the *meta fervidis evitata rotis*. Not even Mr. Cochran can make a classic Brooklands out of that humble site.

Thirty-eight

January 2, 1927

It is still Christmas, let it be remembered, and Christmas customs have not ceased to be topics of the day. And I am reminded of a curious old Welsh custom, which lingered well into my young days, which, for all I know, may still linger. Christmas in the very old days was one of the feasts on which the parish spent all they could afford on lights. There was a Holy Bush, a kind of forerunner of our Christmas Tree, with a reminiscence, perhaps, of the Burning Bush in the wilderness. This was set thick with tapers; the Rood Screen was starred with lights; all the altars and all the glowing images were ablaze with candles. And many lights burnt about the Crib; to simple village eyes accustomed to a dim tallow to get to bed by, if so much illumination as that, the church on Christmas morning must have been a place of splendour and glory, a paradise on earth.

Well, we know that all this sort of thing came to an end with Queen Mary, perhaps because that Sovereign was too much addicted to kindling certain candles of an infernal rather than a celestial nature. Queen Elizabeth, being of similar tastes to Mrs. Pardiggle, and liking her services prettily done, is said to have insisted on the altar in her private chapel being adorned with a crucifix and burning tapers; but, generally, we may say that the candles of the English Church were put out for the next three hundred years, and yet there remained in certain obstinate Welsh heads the lingering notion that at Christmas the parish church should be all ablaze with lights early on Christmas morning; and it may be conjectured that the earliness of the hour was a dim recollection of the Mass in the Night, commonly called Midnight Mass. "O God, Who hast made this most holy night to shine with the glory of the very Light," so went the Collect, and the echo of it was still, it seems, in the Welshmen's ears. At all events, they rose very early, at three or four o'clock, from their farms and cabins on the hillside, and in the valley, and came into the dark church. And then everyone in the assembly drew out a candle and lit it, and one of them read aloud the Gospel stories of the Nativity. I do not think that the parish priest took any part in the ceremony. It was called Plygan, which means, I think, cock-crow. But I am nervous, for I know that Welsh eyes are on me.

There is another side of Christmas. Being the most joyful of seasons, it is, obviously, the time to talk of dreads and terrors, ghosts and goblins.

This truism was recognized, I was glad to see, by the people of East Barnes, and I congratulate the local night watchman on his spectre: a midnight figure, in a dusky cloak, through which a skeleton could be clearly seen. Here you have the genuine ghost of our forefathers, stark and simple, unspoilt by any "psychic" or literary subtleties. Dickens would have loved that phantasm. It is true that he would not have believed in the ghost, but he would have dearly hoped that other people credited every word of the tale. I think that he might have made a Christmas Book out of it, and I believe that a kindly and cheery moral would, somehow, have been found, lurking in the story.

And, as we speak of superstitions, an actor friend and I were discussing professional superstitions about "Macbeth," in relation to Miss Sybil Thorndike's production. From this, easily enough, we got on to the bad luck which the dressing-room holds is bound to follow the breaking of a mirror. I told how I had once endeavoured to shatter this nonsensical belief in the breast of a fellow-actor at the St. James Theatre. Dressing for the first act, he had broken his make-up glass; and he came down to the stage in low spirits. I told him to cheer up, as it was all rubbish, and he looked a little brighter. But between the first and second acts of the play he somehow managed to put his thumb out of joint. I found him in agony, and with an unshakable belief in the ill-luck of mirror breaking.

My friend matched this tale with another. A friend of ours, a well-known actress, found the other day her good-natured though careless Irish servant in floods of tears. The girl confessed, amidst her howlings, that she had broken her mistress's favourite handglass. The kind woman tried to console her: "Don't take it to heart so terribly, Mary. I am afraid you are very careless; still, it can't be helped, and you know the seven years' bad luck comes to me, not to you." The girl's face cleared up as if by magic. She wept no more. "Glory be to God!" she exclaimed, "and is that true? Indeed, I thought the seven years ill-luck would be upon me." Mary was a happy girl again.

The Berlin Correspondent of *The Observer* mentions in last week's issue "Horoscopes on Credit" as among the seasonable and fashionable gifts in the capital. Prognostications, I see, are given fortnightly, and subscriptions are due monthly. And what an excellent plan for setting the old question whether astrology is a veritable science and art or a pack of utter nonsense. I don't know which alternative is true. I have examined most of the astrological almanacks. I find "Labour troubles are threatened during this month." This is true of every month— somewhere. Or I may see that "A Reigning House may be in danger." Of course it may. Or, again, "Owners of factories, etc., are warned to take precautions against accidents." Very rightly, I am sure; but if a workman in a factory at Lowell, Mass., gets his fingers crushed, we are told to wonder. But this is not the way of conviction. I hope that the Horoscopes-on-Hire system of Berlin will succeed in getting something more definite.

Thirty-nine

January 9, 1927

My story of the Irish foxhounds who managed to get from Exmoor to Milford Haven, on their way back to Ireland, has drawn a most interesting letter from a correspondent. He asks, in fact, why I wonder at such a feat as this, since it is nothing to the accomplishment of birds and fishes?

"Have you studied the life history of the eel? It is a marvel to me how the minute elvers, hatched near the Bermudas, find their way as far east as England and the Mediterranean. And how do the females find their way back to the Bermudas, as we are told they do, to spawn there?"

And, indeed, on the face of it, these migrations of eels do seem to cast the journey of the Irish hounds into the shade. But it must be remembered that the dog is a creature very much higher in the scale of being than the eel, and, therefore, all the less likely to possess the purely instinctive faculties. And then, the dog has been domesticated by men for many thousands of years, and therefore again is likely to have lost such faculties as wolves and jackals may still possess. Man has indoctrinated the dog with many of his own laws and customs; he is still, of course, a dog, but he has become a learned dog. And, lastly: was the wild dog, before man had laid his hand on him, migratory at certain seasons, as swallows and salmon are migratory? I should doubt it. And—in the preacher's manner—one word more: it will be noted there is this great distinction between the feat of the foxhounds which made their way from Carlisle to Sussex and of the foxhounds which tried to make their way from Somerset to Ireland, and the migrations of eels, salmon, and swallows. In the latter case you have the fixed, unalterable law of these creatures' existence: in the former you have beasts placed in situations of unforeseen emergency. It is not the law of every dog's existence to return to the place of its birth: if it were, we should have no St. Bernards, Alsatians, or Dalmatians in England; and every kennel would have to keep its puppies all their days.

But I believe Mr. Sleary treats his difficult and perplexed question as lucidly as any of us.

"I have bad dogth find me, Thquire, in a way that made me think whether that dog hadn't gone to another dog, and thed, 'You don't happen to know a perthon of the name of Thlearly, in the Horthe-Riding way—thtout man—game eye?' And whether that dog mightn't have thed, 'Well, I can't thay I know him mythelf, but I know a dog that I think would be likely to be acquainted with him.' And whether that dog mightn't have thought it over and thed, 'Thleary! Thleary! Oh yeth, to be thure! A friend of mine menthioned him to me at one time. I can get you hith addreth directly.'"

It is a distinctly queer thing; but having done with dogs and eels and all such creatures, and being attracted by an address on the Montessori system, delivered lately at the Conference of Educational Associations, I am again moved to quote from "Hard Times." Sissy Jupe, it will be remembered, was a pupil in Mr. Gradgrind's school. The class had been instructed that they must not paper rooms with representations of horses; the reason being that, in fact, horses never walk up and down the sides of rooms. And after that lesson, Sissy Jupe said that she would carpet her room with representations of flowers. The government inspector pointed out that people would walk over them with heavy boots. Whereon Sissy:—

"It wouldn't hurt them, sir. They wouldn't crush and wither, if you please, sir. They would be the pictures of what was very pretty and pleasant, and I would fancy—"

"Ay, ay, ay! But you mustn't fancy," cried the gentleman, quite elated by coming so happily to his point. "That's it! You are never to fancy."

Thus the Gradgrind school of old. At the Montessori School of to-day disciples were informed that Madame Montessori was a good deal peeved—the Americanism is too attractive to be resisted—by the common representations of angels: figures "with the biologically incompatible attributes of both arms and wings!" And then:—

"The power of a child's imagination and credulity enabled it to make an overturned table into a boat, and by bestriding a chair convert it into a horse. Dr. Montessori regarded these things as an illustration of unsatisfied desire. Where the adult resigned himself to his fate the child created an illusion. Dr. Montessori would condemn any mode of education which intended to continue these immature activities on the part of the child."

In other words: "You are never to fancy." What a pity, in the nature of things, Mr. Gradgrind and Madame Montessori could never wed.

To take the taste of all this sad stuff out of my mouth, I have been reading about Harold in "The Golden Age." Harold was found in the tool-shed squatting in an old pig-trough that had been brought in to be tinkered; "and as he rhapsodised, anon he waved a shovel over his head, anon dug it into the ground with the action of those who would urge Canadian canoes. Edward strode in upon him.

"'What rot are you playing now?' he demanded sternly.

"Harold flushed up, but stuck to his pig-trough like a man. 'I'm Jason,' he replied defiantly, 'and this is the Argo. The other fellows are here, too, only you can't see them; and we're just going through the Hellespont, so don't you come bothering.' And once more he plied the wine-dark sea."

I suppose it would take a good deal of argument to persuade Mr. Gradgrind, Madame Montessori, and others that Harold's pig-trough was, in reality, the golden-storied Argo of a magic adventure; while the millionaire's steam yacht is, in reality, often a pig-trough. The rich man finds his way with difficulty into the world of imagination and reality—which is the kingdom of heaven—because he is so strongly tempted to live in the world of actuality.

Forty

January 16, 1927

"It is proposed to erect on the site a block of flats on up-to-date lines." Such is the sentence that has gone forth concerning Abbey Lodge, Regent's Park; and, as usual, when anything old, anything even remotely old, is to be pulled down, I am sorry for it.

Abbey Lodge, of course, is very far from being old in any true sense of the word. It was built, I suppose, somewhere between 1812-20, when the Marleybone Farm and Fields were being turned into Regent's Park, and houses were being erected from the designs of Mr. John Nash the architect of vanished Regent-street and Mr. Decimus Burton. I do not know whether Abbey Lodge is by one or other of these architects, but it is a pleasant example of that preposterous manner which is known as Sham Gothic. There is an unmistakable intention to build in the manner of the fifteenth century; the detail assures you of that; and yet the total effect is grotesquely unlike any conceivable house that could have been built during the period in question. Abbotsford, I suppose, is the most notorious example of this delightful style. A contemporary describes the massive oak carvings of the interior, and mentions that the oak is, in fact, coloured plaster of paris; a fact which, he appears to think, adds a good deal of merit to the design.

It is a pity that some ingenious person does not write a serious— almost serious—"History of Sham Gothic Architecture," adorning it with many plates. And let it be noted, Sham Gothic has its periods like the true Gothic. Abbey Lodge, for example, is distinctly "late," you can trace in it the beginnings of those influences which produced Bad Gothic, and as I am not a technical man I will simply say that the distinction between the two styles is merely this: that the Sham makes you laugh, while the Bad makes you swear. There is not a smile, for example, to be wrung out of the contemplation of the church in the middle of Turnham Green, or the church in Hamilton-terrace, St. John's Wood.

The Golden Age of Sham Gothic was the later half of the eighteenth century. Walpole, Gray, and Mason were its founders, and Walpole was responsible for the masterpiece of the style, the villa at Strawberry Hill. Gray recommends a friend to buy bits of coloured glass to stick into windows, giving these fragments a "Gothic aspect" by turning them cornerwise; and there is a certain "stucco paper," representing arches and niches, which is "rather pretty and nearly Gothic." Then, there is Mason's hero, Alcander, who soothes his sorrows by landscape gardening and romantic architecture:—

Let every structure needful for a farm
Arise in castle-semblance; the huge barn
Shall with a broad portcullis awe the gate
Where Ceres entering, o'er the flail-proof floor
In golden triumph rides; some tower rotund
Shall to the pigeons and their callow young
Safe roost afford.

And the ice-house and the dairy are to look exactly like "a time struck abbey." Long ago I remember seeing something of the kind attempted on a more modest scale. Behind the wall of a Gunnersbury villa, another wall, with turrets about it, arose. It depicted a fragment of a ruined medieval castle, and it was executed in clinkers.

Mr. C. W. Bailey, headmaster of the Holt School, Liverpool, has supplied a noble antidote to the Gradgrind-Montessori nonsense we were discussing last week. "No one," he told the Northern Education Conference, "has taught or lived with little children without realising how strong is their power of make-believe. Fairy tales have no difficulties for them, for they are themselves the fairies. To break the iridescent bubble of their fancy by the intrusion of dull, disturbing fact is a sorry sport for adults. ... Let them live, in imagination, a whole cycle of lives." and, after all, if we live well, we continue the treatment in later years. We make-believe that there were people called Hamlet, Falstaff, Sancho Panza, Mrs. Gamp, and Mr. Micawber: we spend many hours in reading about these people; year after year we follow the strange adventures of some of them on the stage. Nay, we are infinitely more interested in them than in very many of our friends and acquaintances. Which would you rather receive: a letter from Jones to the effect that he got home all right on Tuesday, and it looks as if it would turn to rain— or a great Micawber chapter, which by some mischance was omitted during the progress of "David Copperfield"? I admit that it is highly curious that some of our most vital, most joyous, and profitable hours are spent with people who have no existence in reality; but so it is. It is a part of the great paradox of humanity.

...

One night on circuit, Talfourd, who was the judge's marshall, advised his chief, Baron Martin, to read "Measure for Measure." The next morning Talfourd asked the judge how he had enjoyed the play. "I cannot say that I think much of it," replied Martin. "It contains atrociously bad law. I am of opinion that your friend Shakespeare is an over-rated man." No doubt the judge was right; from his technical standpoint. But the odd thing is that many people try to prove that Shakespeare was a learned man, an exact scholar in all the realms of human knowledge. Ben Jonson knew better; but we will not heed Ben. We will not even heed our own common sense, which ought to tell us, plainly enough, Belch and Aguecheek are not Illyrian names, and that a ninth century prince could not desire to go to a university of sixteenth century foundation.

Forty-One

January 23, 1927

It is some time, I think, since we have heard about the fairies. The last tale of them, if I remember, was the very singular experience narrated by that well-known writer, Miss Sommerville: how she and a brother, when they were children together, heard a sudden burst of wonderful music, and ran out to find "the German band"—and found that there was no band to be seen, and that no one but themselves had heard anything. This is strange enough, and it has drawn forth a story which is stranger still.

My correspondent heard it from the late Colonel Vaughan, of Courtfield, Ross, the head of an ancient family and brother of Cardinal Vaughan, Father Bernard Vaughan, and other distinguished ecclesiastics of the Roman Catholic Church. Here is the tale:—

"In the late 'seventies or early 'eighties, Colonel Vaughan (or Captain Vaughan as he then was) rented for the sake of certain sporting rights in a large house near the town of Newport, in the County Mayo, Ireland. Being a Catholic, he got on with the people very well, and being an English gentleman of position, he also got on with the squireens, or Irish gentry. He was always entertaining and being entertained. It was when he was returning from one of these dinners late one night that the curious thing happened. He had driven through the town of Newport and had just come to a part of the road where there was a large field, in the midst of which stood a 'tut-mill,' or 'tuck-mill.' When he came to this place the horse stopped dead and refused to budge. Looking over the stone fence, the Captain, to his surprise, saw at a distance of about a hundred yards, a number of undersized people formed up in a ring, and one in the centre holding up what appeared to be a piece of burning wood with sparks flying upwards. The Captain shouted, 'What is the matter?' Nobody seemed to take any notice, and the circular movement or dance continued. Captain Vaughan scented political outrage; whipped round the unwilling horse, and turned back to Newport. He went straight to the police barracks and told the sergeant what he had seen. The sergeant, to his surprise, refused point-blank to return with him to the field, saying that what had been seen there was no concern of his, and the affair had better be left alone. The Captain thereupon drove home, and, passing the field, found it quite deserted."

Of course, my correspondent adds, the jocular made a point of the fact that Captain Vaughan had "dined." But in the first place, as he says, the Captain was a singularly temperate and well-balanced man, and secondly, people do not begin to "see things" till they are on the verge of delirium tremens. And, anticipating another objection, I would say, on my part, that while English country gentlemen may sometimes overcolour their stories of fish, and mares, and birds, they do not invent wild fantasies of the unknown world. In other words, Captain Vaughan was not a deliberate liar.

But what are we to make of his story? He might have been subject to an hallucination; this is possible, but highly improbable, all the circumstances of the case being considered. Or, again; his first impression might have been approximately correct; the men in a ring might have been seditious peasants who were practising traditional Irish dances after the serious business of their secret assembly had been transacted. I believe that dislike of the English connection and a love of ancient Irish sports and dances were often associated together. But then, there is the word, "undersized": that is distinctly puzzling. Captain Vaughan could not have thought that the beings he saw were children; since children do not plot political outrages. And then, again; are the Mayo peasants generally dwarfish? If they are not, and I believe they are not, did it not strike the observer as curious that all the supposed conspirators were men under the usual height? "Undersized," I take it, implies a height between four and four and a half feet; which, I think, is about the stature of the African pygmies.

And this talk of things seen and experienced in Ireland reminds me of a talk I had the other day with a well-known man of letters. I was telling him the true and very horrible story of the Irish peasant who burnt his wife alive, because he believed her to be a fairy changeling. "There is only one cure," said my friend. "Educate them; they will soon stop believing in all that nonsense." But will they? The necromancers are educated people. The people who have their horoscopes drawn, who employ crystal-gazers and palmists and geomancers are often highly educated. And, only a week ago, when Mr. F. Mitchell-Hedges, the well-known explorer, was held up and "robbed" by some wild young jokers, he was most distressed at losing—as he thought—a case containing four specimens of rare human heads, which had been shrunk by Indians by a secret process. "I have always looked upon them as a mascot," said Mr. Mitchell-Hedges, "and carried them about everywhere." Now, I am sure that Mr. Mitchell-Hedges is highly educated. But a mascot is, in plain English, a talisman; object endowed with an occult virtue by which good fortune is secured to its possessor. What is there to choose between belief in talismans and belief in fairies? I had rather believe in the Little People dancing in a ring than believe that the idiotic Rite and Ceremony called "Touch Wood" can have any influence on the fate of men.

A London dealer has in his possession an old stained-glass window from Staffordshire which displays the characters "Mary R." and something that looks like "July 27," both written with a diamond. Mary Queen of Scots is supposed to be the author of the inscription. If so, she anticipated our modern script by three hundred years.

Forty-two [1]

January 30, 1927

Disappearances are always attractive. We have had strong and recent experience in support of that proposition. A very fine example of the mysterious disappearance was given the other day by Mr. H. W. Walbrook, writing in the "Evening Standard." "Almost twenty-three years ago, a tenant of Clifford's Inn walked out one night at about 11:00 and told the porter he was going to post a letter. Next morning his laundress found the bed unslept in and the gas full on. The tenant never returned, nor was anything ever heard of him. His goods were eventually sold, and the porter bought a watercolour picture."

I gather from Mr. Walbrook's account that the missing man had followed some regular daily occupation, in which he was associated with other men. Now, I was talking a few weeks ago with just such a man. He has followed, with success, just such a daily occupation, in which he is associated with other men. And he said to me: "Do you know that I've been in this business for twenty-seven years, and I hate it now worse than I did on my first day in the office?" Well, my friend is a married man with children; the tenant of the old Inn was a bachelor. I find no difficulty in supposing that, as this man posted his letter in Fleet-street, he was suddenly seized with a thrill of loathing and disgust at the thought of the office and its daily routine, and of the constant faces of Brown, Jones, and Henderson, his associates. He realised for the first time how utterly he hated it all—and resolved that he would have done with it forever. He was a middle-aged man when he vanished. I believe him to be still alive and happy, a street watchman, cooking his steaks over the glowing brazier, well sheltered in a strong wigwam from all the bitter blasts of life.

It seems that whimsicality, pure and simple, is the explanation of the following case of disappearance—if we can call it a disappearance—which has been sent me by a friend:—

"One afternoon," the story goes, "in the 'twenties or the 'thirties of the last century, a gentleman was driven up to the White Horse Cellars, Piccadilly, in a coach. He paid the coachman, carried a heavy valise into the hotel, and ordered a room and dinner, with breakfast for next morning.

---

[1] Due to the poor state of the source material, this installment has been truncated.

He paid his bill regularly every morning, staying at the hotel for twenty years. One morning he paid his bill, went out, and was never seen again."

There are no difficulties here. The gentleman had probably tired of Tutbury or Lhasa or Lunel—where they make liqueur wine with the muscat flavour—before he alighted at the White Horse Cellars. Tiring in due course of the White Horse Cellars, he took comfortable furnished rooms in Islington where he died years after, leaving a nephew in the country a very considerable fortune.

They are talking of moving London Stone—and I hope to goodness that their talk may have no issue in action. "Melbourne! thou should'st be living at this hour: England hath need of thee." In some ages of the world it may be necessary to move London Stone—I inclined to doubt it—but at present we certainly need to remember Lord Melbourne's great counsel in a query: "Why can't you leave it alone?"

As it is, London Stone is not in its original position. It has crossed Candlewick—now Cannon-street.

"On the south side of this high street, near unto the channel [the gutter] is pitched upright a great stone called London Stone, fixed in the ground very deep, fastened with bars of iron, and otherwise so strongly sat that if carts do run against it through negligence the wheels be broken and the stone itself unshaken."

Thus sixteenth-century Stow. But in 1742, in the mid-eighteenth century, an age which should have known better, the Stone was moved from the south to the north side of the street, and it was disturbed again in 1798, narrowly escaping destruction. It was said to be a nuisance and an obstruction. If you look at things from a certain point of view, St. Paul's Cathedral is clearly an obstruction, if not exactly a nuisance— though, for my part, I detest Stainer and Anglican chants.

Forty-three

February 6, 1927

The old theory about London Stone, which we were discussing last week, was that it was a *milliarium*, a central milestone from which the Roman roads of Britain radiated and distances were calculated. It may well have been that, but, to the fascinating theory of Mr. Alfred Watkins, of Hereford, it had its use and purpose a long, long time before ever the Romans touched the soil of Britain.

"Long before any London town came into being on the Thames bank," writes Mr. Watkins, "before there were any towns or villages, or even houses as we know them now, primitive man in the hunting phase made tracks across country to get his supplies of salt or flints, or to barter skins for pots. He did it by sighting from a hilltop, and, later on, planting certain types of marks on the face of the land to indicate what became an organised track. Mounds these were for the most part, and about London they were placed on Parliament Hill, in Bunhill Fields, at Primrose Hill. ... And, in between, were lesser marks, unusual looking stones placed on the wayside to give assurance to the traveller that he was on the right track. Of these few are left in London; best known is London Stone in Cannon-street." And so, in clamorous Cannon-street, prehistoric man beckons to us.

A lady, who says she is a native of the west of Ireland, sends me her reading of the sight that Colonel Vaughan, of Courtfield, saw one night in Mayo: undersized men dancing in a ring by the light of a torch held up by one in the centre. "The group of persons seen were either occupied drilling secretly, or (what is far more likely) in the brewing or smuggling of illicit liquor and their strange conduct may have been the result of indulgence or to alarm the Colonel. Their dwarfish aspect was due, perhaps, to deceptive light and the home-made cut of their garments. They were observed near a tumulus or 'Danish Fort,' a haunt of fairy folk, and therefore a place to be avoided, and, for that very reason, useful to conceal an illicit still or contraband of spirits."

Well: this explanation seems to me probable enough, and I think it should always be our practice to accept the more probable rather than the less probable theory; provided, of course, that the former fairly accounts for the facts. I still hesitate a little over "undersized," since I am inclined to think that the torchlight would rather exaggerate than diminish objects seen by it, still, my correspondent may well have hit on the veritable explanation of a queer story.

And here comes another tale of "undersized" people, of a very different order. This correspondent tells me what she saw at Saffron Walden, which she visited about six years ago with the Essex Archaeological Society.

"A halt was made at mid-day to enable us to eat our lunch in a beautiful old garden in the town. I sat down in an arbour facing a broad grass walk, with a short yew hedge, and began to take my lunch and to read the morning paper. Suddenly, I became aware of something moving along the path, away from me, and upon looking closely I saw it to be two dwarfish figures, about 2 feet 6 inches tall, and clothed, one in black and one in rust colour, in the traditional tight fitting jerkin and hose of a gnome. Although I longed to follow these curious little creatures, I was strangely rooted to the spot, and could only watch them moving farther and farther away, until they reached the garden wall, where they suddenly disappeared, whether through it or over it I could not tell. I did not mention what I had seen to any of my fellow-excursionists, several of whom were sitting nearby, where their outlook commanded the view of the path along which the gnomes had walked. None of them spoke of having seen anything unusual."

Here, I believe, we have a clear case of hallucination, the English for which is "seeing things." The commonest cause of hallucination is, I suppose, excessive alcohol, with its resulting delirium. The "things seen" are not always terrifying or horrible. A doctor told me of a D. T. patient of his who seemed quiet and reasonable in every respect, save for a nervous trick of scraping the carpet with his foot. It turned out that he was putting out lighted cigarettes—which were not there. Then, again, extreme fatigue may have similar results: some of our soldiers, tired, indeed almost to death, during the famous retreat from Mons, where bewildered by spectral chairs and tables and burning candles, which appeared on the road before them. Yet another way of hallucination is that of the crystal-gazer and the ink-gazer. And, of course, the vision of the non-existent may be apparently spontaneous, as appears to be the case with my correspondent's experience. But there is one feature common to the results of all the varying methods; and that is that the thing seen is a projection, an apparent externalisation, of something within the seer's consciousness or sub-consciousness. There were no lighted cigarettes on the carpet, there were no burning candles on the road from Mons, and—as I hold—there were no gnomes in the Saffron

Walden garden. Likely enough, they came out of an illustrated fairytale which the lady had read in childhood, had forgotten, consciously, and remembered, subconsciously.

The occultists, I believe, maintain that there is much more than mere symbolism in the halo, the ring of light depicted about the heads of the saints. Each one of us, these sages declare, has an aura about him, and there are those to whom these auras are visible. Indeed, in a certain famous cathedral town, the parlour-maid at the Deanery had this gift. She used to shudder, as she told Miss Dean, when she opened the door to one of the canons—a well-known figure of twenty years ago. His aura, as she saw it, was of a dirty purplish colour, splotched with patches of bilious yellow.

It is curious to know that one of the most thorough-paced blackguards that ever lived, Benvenuto Cellini, claimed the possession of a halo: "a resplendent light about his head," which appeared at dawn and sunset, and showed best when the grass was wet with dew. Benvenuto considered that his halo was a signal mark of the divine approval of his virtuous life, but in this he must have been mistaken. If he had a halo at all, it must have been even worse than the canon's—a sort of post-impressionist halo.

Forty-four

February 13, 1927

Commenting on the dainty folk of Oswaldtwistle, who desire to change the name of their town, a writer asks—after Shakespeare—"What's in a name?" and asks that people do not flock to Paradise in Somerset. No; but the existence of such a place-name throws a curious light on a very ancient enigma. Readers of the old romance will remember that King Arthur's end is clouded with a strange doubt. The legend tells how he was borne away by the Queen of Faerie to Avalon, the Isle of the Blessed, but some men say, adds the romancer, that he was taken to Glastonbury, and there buried. How are we to account for the two versions of the passing of Arthur?

In my opinion, the matter fell out thus, Avalon, which means Applegarth, was the Celtic name of the place which the Saxon conquerors called Glastinga Burg. But Avalon also signified the Celtic pre-Christian paradise, "the glassy isle beyond the waves of ocean." It was to this Avalon that the early legend spiritually translated King Arthur. It was a later, rationalising age which buried him bodily in the other Avalon which is Glastonbury. And so, if ours were a myth-making age, we could imagine similar confusions tracing their origin to yet another place in Somerset—Paradise. But the only myths we can devise are squalid, malevolent, crazy. They are little likely to concern themselves with either Paradise, on high or below.

The correspondent who explained the Irish version of Colonel Vaughan by poteen, and the revels consequent on its making, sends me a curious note on the similarity she has observed between the natives of Ireland and the natives of Ceylon. "In 1883," she writes, "I was walking along a Cork footpath beside my English governess, when our attention was attracted by two persons standing on either side of a donkey, and passing a small child beneath it from one to the other. The governess ask them why they did this, and then hurried away. The men had told her it was a cure for whooping cough."

"In 1916, I was passing along the Perandenirga Road, Kandy, and I saw a baby being passed under the body of an elephant. My guide explained that the child had stomach trouble."

"The belief in transmigration of souls is, of course, pretty universal in Ceylon, but it was strange to hear a man of West Kerry explain the local dislike of killing hares by the question 'How would I know but that hare might be my grandmother?' And fifty years ago there was a Connaught gander who followed the farmer, its owner, about like a dog. The local 'wise man' declared that it was the farmer's father, come back to earth, and arrangements were made to drown the bird. But they miscarried, and the gander is said to have lived to a good old age."

These coincidences of belief in Cork and Kandy are certainly most interesting but I should not be at all surprised to hear that Chinese villagers and Australian Blackfellows held similar beliefs and cured infantile maladies by similar processes. The Lost Paradise myth of the venerable head of Bran Vendigeid in the Welsh Mabinogion is an extraordinary legend, and the Red Indians of North America have a Lost Paradise myth which is very like it. The singular conception of a decapitated head being the lord and ruler of the household is common in both stories.

At Isleworth, a week or two ago, a woman left her baby in the cot with her dog, as usual, at the foot of the cot, guarding the child. When the mother returned, both baby and dog had vanished. She rushed out into the garden, and the dog jumped up from the door of his kennel, barked, and ran back to the kennel. Inside it was the baby, fast asleep. A neighbour told her what had happened. She had seen the baby crawling down the path which led to the stream at the bottom of the garden. The dog began to jump about the child, then it turned it around, bumping it with his head till he had pushed it into the kennel, and he mounted guard outside.

So far Isleworth, now let us travel to Bulawayo. Here, also quite recently, a honey-bird lured a native to a tree, where the man was struck by a deadly snake and died in a few minutes. And the "Daily Mail" representative, who sends the news, says that "this lends colour to the belief that a honey-bird sometimes maliciously leads to a lion, leopard, or snake, instead of a store of wild honey." But this imputation on the bird was refuted by another correspondent, who explains the innocence of its design. "My brother," he says, "had an experience of this sort. A honey-bird led him to a tree and fluttered round its stem, where a snake was coiled. My brother shot the snake, and the honey-bird cheerfully settled on its nest." The honey-bird, in short, wishes to be rid of a dangerous enemy, not to play unkind practical jokes on man.

And my design inciting these instances from Isleworth and Bulawayo is to show how absurdly we define man as a reasonable animal. The ratiocinative faculty is by no means the differentia of man. It is shared by many other animals. The Isleworth dog reasoned, in a very elegant manner, that Johnny was making for the stream, that Johnny was a baby, that no babies can swim, that no babies know that they cannot swim, therefore, that Johnny would be drowned if he fell into the water. So the honey-bird rattled off its syllogisms in "Barbara":—

> The creature is a snake.
> All snakes eat honey birds.
> Therefore, this creature eats honey birds.

And then:—

> That creature is a man.
> All men kill snakes.
> Therefore, that man kills snakes.

Thus, both in the case of the dog and the case of the bird, you have examples of pure ratiocination. There can be no question of instinct, which is always general, common to the whole race, and exercised in compulsory racial movements, such as the migration of salmon, eels, and swallows. But dogs, as a race, are not endowed with an instinctive knowledge of the fact that babies are unable to swim. And that other proposition, that men kill snakes, must have been established for the honey-bird by a process of induction. It is, be it observed, a probable proposition only; sometimes it is the man, not the snake, who perishes. True instinct does not deal with probable propositions; it is a universal imperative.

Forty-five

February 20, 1927

St. George remains on the new Calendar, but St. Valentine goes, and I should much like to know the principle by which the fate of the two saints was determined. For, with respect to St. George, it must be frankly said that we know nothing whatever about him, and, what is more, the compilers of the Roman Breviary who were not over critical, knew nothing whatever about him. His service is composed of what is technically known as the Common of Martyrs, verses and responses which may be used for any martyrs. There is no attempt at a legend, not a hint of the Dragon. To the authorities responsible for the Breviary, St. George was evidently, nothing more than a name.

St. Valentine stands on a far firmer ground. His feast is honoured by the insertion of a brief sermon of St. Augustine for whom the saint was clearly an historical personage. Says St. Augustine on the anniversary of the blessed martyr Valentine, "The Church rejoices in his fate and bids us to follow in his steps. For if we suffer with him we shall also be glorified with him. Two circumstances are proposed for our consideration: the remorseless savagery of the torturer, the unconquered patience of the Martyr. Let us abhor the one and imitate the other."

It seems as if a saint who could be thus extolled by St. Augustine, that great Doctor of the whole Church, were worthy of a place in the Calendar of the English Church. And I cannot think that the innocent tokens which are called Valentines constitute any objection to the position of the saint. For many ages, St. Bartholomew was chiefly known to Londoners in connection with a famous, though a frivolous fair, but that was nothing against St. Bartholomew. And, by the way, "O Saptentia" still marks December 16, though the Revisers of 1927 have added the doubtful dignity of brackets. But why did the original compilers of the Prayer Book place these two words in the calendar? O Sapentia is the first of a series of antiphons proceeding Christmas known as "The Great Oes." There was no provision whatever for the singing of these antiphons in the Prayer Book: the inclusion of the opening words of one of them in the Calendar seems a puzzling circumstance. I have sometimes wondered whether our forefathers knew that it was time to kill the Christmas pig when the clerks began to sing "the Great Oes," and whether our benevolent Reformers abolishing O Saptentia, O Adonai, O Radix Jesse, and the rest of them, set the words of the first down in the Calendar lest a bewildered generation should lack brawn at Christmas.

The lady who should be known as my special correspondent in Fairyland tells me that in her opinion, belief in the People is now absolutely dead in Ireland. It may be so but I should doubt it. There is an old theory, cited by my correspondent that the fairy legends of Ireland are founded on the fact that the short dark race, who were in Ireland before the Celts, retreated from the conquerors into the wild places of the island, hiding in the woods like the Asiki—the Little People of Africa—hollowing out for themselves caves in the mountains. I think that the notion has a great deal to commend it. It accounts for many of the fairy stories, and it is well to note that ancient traditions are rarely, if ever, wholly false, though they are often highly decorated. And, to put it boldly, how do we know that this little dark race is not still in hiding, up and down Ireland? It is all very well to answer, "I never saw them when I was in Ireland." But Colonel Vaughan, of Courtfield, had a very strong belief that he did see them, when he was in Ireland.

Sir Trevor Dawson, Knight President of the Knights of the Round Table Club, thinks that the excavations in the Roman Amphitheatre at Caerleon-on-Usk will lead to valuable information bearing on the Arthurian cycle. I hope he is right, but I do not quite see how a Roman monument can throw much light on a Celtic-Anglo-Norman mythos. I have just been saying that ancient tradition is never false. But the great cycle of Arthurian romance is not a highly decorated version of an early legend about King Arthur. It is that, no doubt, but it has half-a-dozen other things as well; it draws from the most various sources, and the Romance writers were utterly "unscrupulous." Thus certain orders are attributed to St. Columba in an ancient Irish text: in one of the Percival romances these orders are put into the mouth of King Arthur.

And then, again, there is the missionary element in the Arthurian cycle, the very late tradition of Britain evangelised by St. Joseph of Arimathea. There is also the Grail motive, which is a decorated legend of the fall of the Celtic Church. It was the skill of the thirteenth century romance writer which grouped these and other elements around King Arthur, with whom they had originally no connection whatever. In a word, King Arthur is not an historical monarch like King Alfred: he is a magnet, attracting to himself all the legends and tales that were current in the world of 1200.

Forty-six

February 27, 1927

We were talking the other day about seeing things, more sonorously known as hallucination. I mentioned, by the way, several sorts of hallucination that produced by intense fatigue, that which results from strong potations, and, lastly, the hallucinatory images which appear to the scryers, or crystal-gazers. A correspondent, who simply signs himself "A Rosicrucian," is not inclined to admit that the things seen in the crystal are hallucinations. He says that they are objective realities, so far objective that they have been photographed. In proof cf which, he sends me a reproduction of a photograph of a vision in the crystal—which, I am bound to say, looks to me like a reproduction of an engraving of the 1760-1790.

But my Rosicrucian correspondent also directed my attention to Mr. Theodore Bestermann's treatise on crystal-gazing, in support of the objective theory of the visions seen by scryers. So far as I can see, Mr. Bestermann holds that the visions are hallucinatory. His final conclusion and definition of the crystal-gazer's art is that it is "a method of bringing into consciousness of the scryer by means of a speculum through one or more of his senses the content of his subconsciousness, of rendering him more susceptible to the reception of telepathically transmitted concepts, and of bringing into operation a latent and unknown faculty of perception." The vision, in other words, is in the soul of the seer, not in the crystal or in a pool of ink.

Mr. Bestermann, in the course of his work, relates the extraordinary experience of Sir Joseph Barnby, the well-known composer. Sir Joseph was visiting Lord and Lady Radnor at Longford Castle. In the house-party was a Miss A., a notable scryer. One day, she looked into the crystal and described her vision to Sir Joseph. The seer saw a room, as it were, through an open door. In it, she saw a lady, drying her hands on a towel. The lady was tall, dark, slightly foreign in appearance, and with rather "an air" about her. Sir Joseph Barnby found this an excellent description of his wife, and asked for details as to her dress. Miss A. said the dress was of serge, and described the braid trimming. "This," said Sir Joseph Barnby, "threw me off the scent, as before I had started for Longford my wife expressed her regret that she had not a serge dress with her."

But the lady of the vision was, indeed Lady Barnby. Sir Joseph rejoined her at Eastbourne, and to his amazement saw her wearing the serge dress, made exactly as it had been described by the seer. Lady Barnby's statement tells how the serge dress was ordered the day after Sir Joseph left for Longford, and how she came to be washing her hands in an hotel bedroom with the door open: "I do not suppose," Lady Barnby adds, "I have ever done such a thing before or since." And sixteen months after the event, Miss A. pointed out Lady Barnby to Sir Joseph at a London concert, "You will remember my seeing a lady in her bedroom while looking in the crystal, that is the lady I saw."

Now all the dates in this case were carefully noted at the time; and, to add it to the strangeness of it all, it appears that the vision was prophetic. It was seen by Miss A. at least half a day before the event. Another queer point is the absolute triviality of the event, that is, the fact that Lady Barnby for once washed her hands in a room with an open door. And then, again, note the odd limitation of the range of the vision. Miss A. saw in the crystal exactly so much of the room as she would have seen if she had been actually standing just outside the open door. So here you have a faculty which transcends both space and time, but is baffled by a piece of painted wood. And—this is the most important—telepathy as an explanation is completely out of court. When Miss A. saw the vision in the crystal at Longford, Lady Barnby at Eastbourne had no notion that she would be washing her hands in a hurry some hours later.

A good many years ago I had a talk with the late Georg Brandes. We were discussing the very ingenious theory that Shakespeare was an undecided, hesitating, infirm of purpose, somewhat timorous individual, the ground for this theory being that such typical characters as Hamlet and Macbeth are shown as incapable of bold, determined, resolved action. Brandes would have none of it, and he was no doubt right in his rejection. If Shakespeare had been a Hamlet, he would not have made a fortune in the wild riot of Elizabethan London; he would not have been one of the little syndicate who took up land and built the theatre by Southwark; he would not have settled it down in Stratford, solid and content. No doubt the irresolute man interested and attracted him as a topic, as a character to put into a play. But I think it would be unsafe to conclude that the author who likes writing about bloody and murderous pirates is himself a pirate at heart. It is probable, indeed, that if he actually saw the scuppers—I have no notion what scuppers are—awash with blood, he would become extremely unwell.

...

"According to a servant who has lived in the house for 28 years, there are two ghosts—one, a lumbering, tramping, shuffling thing, prowling about the upstairs rooms, and the other, a demure little old woman haunting the back garden." Thus the "Daily Mail" description of the Haunted House of The Week, and, as one somewhat curious in ghosts, I cannot say that I am much impressed. I think a gourmet of ghosts would say that these phantoms are "of the old game"; the technique is that of a Christmas Number of the eighteen-sixties. But, passing from the haunters to the haunted house, here I find real merit. This house, a "creeper-clad" residence on Kew Green, was built in the reign of George I.—an excellent date. And the owner, who lives in it and is a member of the Richmond Borough Council, has not yet made up his mind as to how many rooms it contains, over and above the secret passages in the panelling. This is sumptuous: a detail which almost brings the old house at Kew into the magnificent category of Glamis Castle.

Addenda

Le Morte D'Arthur

December 17, 1933

The wise are wary in dealing in superlatives. It may be due to the Fall, as Mr. G. K. Chesterton (I think) would say; but it is dangerous to predicate perfection of any mortal work. But, bearing this in mind, I must say that I think the "Shakespeare Head Press Malory" is very nearly perfect. The sumptuous paper, that is thick enough to be rich, and not too thick for comfortable handling, the pure and clear font, the balance of the page, with its nicely observed proportion of text and margin, the fine rubrication, the "colore di fiamma" of the binding: all seem to me of the best and choicest. It has all the reverence and devotion of a Missal; and such a show is well fitting for this rare old book, which represents for Englishmen one of the noblest legends of the world. The romances of King Arthur and the Round Table, of Lancelot and Guinevere, of Percival and Galahad, and of the Holy Grail were first written in the French of the twelfth and thirteenth centuries. For the France of to-day, these romances are literary and antiquarian curiosities; the preserve, or almost, of experts; and matter for discussion and argument of the intensest interest—to experts. But so far as I am aware, the matter of the romances has hardly entered at all into the literary life-blood of France. The tales have not been made of the general consciousness. The modern French writer does not feel them even vaguely in the background of his dreams. To him, the Percival and the Merlin, the Queste and the Grand Saint Graal are no more present than the poems of Caedmon to an English novelist.

It is our good fortune that, through the blest work of Sir Thomas Malory, King Arthur and the Holy Grail, Sir Lancelot and Queen Guinevere have been children's books and grown-up books, too, for the last four hundred years. It is true that Roger Ascham cursed Malory, but God before cursed him. Malory and all the legends he collected and collated are part of the living substances of English literature. With better fortune Tennyson might have renewed their life in a modern epic—though it seems hard to believe in the possibility of a modern epic. He began well with the fragment "Morte d'Arthur," but then, towards the middle of his life, some faintly scented delicate breath from vicarage drawing-rooms swooned upon him, and he mingled the decorous image of the Prince Consort with the vision of King Arthur; and all was lost. Indeed, he said himself that he meant the Order of the Knights of the Round Table to symbolise Liberal institutions. After which, there is, clearly, nothing to be said.

The chief consequence, then, of this new-old story of King Arthur and his Knights and the Grail is in the fact that it is one of the greatest stories in the world, and that is part of our literary consciousness. But, that granted, I am free to aver that I quite appreciate its other aspect, as a golden quarry of research and argument and learned dreams. To catalogue the various theories that have been formed, merely glancing at each one in passing, is in itself a rich entertainment. Old Rossetti, the Italian exile, father of Dante Gabriel, held that all the romances of chivalry were elaborate allegorical treatises against the Pope. According to this school, when you read in your romance book of a Distressed Damosel, you are to understand that she symbolises the hidden church of the true believers, which turns out on examination to be the Albigensian sect—and though the Albigenses were savagely persecuted, they were not really nice or wise people. Then, Wolfram von Eschenbach, author of the "Parzival," as "Templesiens." This was enough and more than enough for another set of researchers, who forthwith made the romances a manifesto of the Order of the Temple, and incorporated all the tiresome twaddle that has been written about the Templars with their theory of the legend of the Grail. A more modern author, Miss Weston, expended vast and conscientious labour in proving, as she thought, that the Grail legends and tales were built upon the ritual of a Gnostic sect, which has persisted in Wales up to the eleventh century. She found also traces of sexual symbolism and of a Fertility mythos. Still later, a gentleman, whose name I do not recollect, has derived a whole cycle from the Greek mythology. And a favourite sport has been, and still is, to regard all the Christian and sacramental elements in the romances as impertinent excrescences on a pagan Irish story about a miraculous feeding bowl.

And, in a way, all these vanities and vexations are but tributes to the splendour and the majesty of the text whereon they comment. It is the mark of a great book to have a wilderness of ardent and ingenious nonsense written about it.

A Noble Malory

February 4, 1934

The judicious booklover now has his Malory complete. All that remains for him to do is to choose some suitable moated grange as a habitation for the wonderful book in its sumptuous edition.

In a brief notice of the first volume, I indicated some aspects of the problem of the Arthurian legend and its origin. It must be said that, after all the exertions of the learned, and ingenious, the problem remains unsolved, and, in all probability, unsolvable. The raw material was, undoubtedly, of the Celtic stock. It is clear, also, that the Anglo-Norman poets and romance writers did not receive it as a compact and coherent legend, which only required to be translated into French. Rather, they received an incoherent mass of legends; some British or Welsh, some Irish, and some, no doubt, of mixed origin. There was an element, and a strong one of pagan folklore; there was another element of ecclesiastical legend and legendary history. Chretien de Troyes left his tale unfinished, and though he mentions the Grail, we do not know in what sense he used the word, or what powers he assigned to the vessel. On the other hand, Borron, writing soon after Chretien, tells what is, practically, a missionary story of the evangelisation of Britain. Every country wished to trace back its Christianity to an apostolic, or at least, a scriptural origin. Borron fixed on St. Joseph of Arimathea as the Apostle of the Britons; and it is interesting to compare his legend with the parallel Provençal story of the Saintes Maries de la mer. Borron, no doubt, had heard of what we may call the folklore Grail, the magic feeding vessel of the pagans. But with him, the Grail is wholly sanctified. It provides a feast, it is true, but the feast consists only of a fish, and those familiar with the Ichthus symbolism will know what is implied.

These two poems, one by Chretien, the other by Borron, are the earliest examples of the Anglo-Norman cycle of the Grail. It is likely enough, though it cannot be certain, that Chretien set out to retell the old story of Percival, his Exile, Return and Vengeance—a majestic variant of the tale of the Ugly Duckling—without a thought of any special Christian significance in his story or in the Grail Vessel, which he barely mentions. Borron, on the other hand, has not heard of Percival, and writes this missionary narrative rather in the manner of a monk engaged to enrich the Legendarium of his monastery.

Between these two extremes the Romances move, mingling the two motives, Christian and Pagan; but resolving them at last into the great mystery of the book of Galahad; a romance of the very heart of the Faith.

FROM THE POST-BAG.

January 3, 1937

Dr. Johnson and the Occult.

Your representative is mistaken in stating that a " young woman bamboozled Dr. Johnson by cracking her joints." The doctor was a member of the committee which investigated the affair of the Cock-lane ghost. He drew up their report, which appeared in the newspapers and in the " Gentleman's Magazine." The last sentence of this document runs:—" It is, therefore, the opinion of the whole assembly that the child has some art of making or counterfeiting a particular noise, and that there is no agency of any higher cause."—A. MACHEN, *Amersham, Bucks.*

HOW LONDON LIVED IN 1827.

A Jolly Place, but Dirty—and Small—Night Life Without "Dora"—Old Bailey Horrors.
By ARTHUR MACHEN

May 20, 1927

A good many of us, I am very sure, living, as we say, in a world of racket and hurry and change and confusion, wish we had been alive a hundred years ago when everything was peaceful and placid, and people took things in a leisurely way, when there were very few miles of railway, no telegraph, no motorcars, no wireless.

Why, Mr. Pickwick began his immortal pilgrimage on May 13, 1827: it was the golden age; and romance and adventure without rush were still to be encountered on the English roads.

I feel all this myself; and I am quite sure that the people who read the first number of the "Standard" in their coffee houses said to one another:—

"Well, sir, we live in very singular times."

"You are quite right, sir. I never know what I shall read next."

"I have the best Authority for saying that the Greeks in Athens have been forced to surrender to the Turkish forces. What's to become of them?" "Damn the Greeks, sir, that's what I say, damme! I say, let's mind our own business and let the Greeks mind theirs. What's going to be the next move of the Irish Catholics, that's what I want to know? The Duke won't trust'em; not he."

"I think you're very right, sir. The Duke's an Irishman himself, and knows his countrymen. Ha! Ha!"

"It's all very well to be merry, gentleman; but I have to tell you that it's my firm belief that the country is on the brink of a precipice. What do we know about Mr. Canning. I say he's a Whig at heart, and what's a Whig but a traitor in disguise. The fellow's mother was nothing better than a play actress."

And there were all sorts of startling things outside of politics to be talked of in 1827. London Bridge was being rebuilt. A steam coach, carrying a number of passengers, had gone up Highgate Hill at the rate of thirteen miles an hour. The setting of spring-guns and a man-traps had been forbidden by Act of Parliament. Some people wanted to make it lawful to sell game; there was a restless spirit abroad. A peer asked from his place in Parliament why an alderman who could buy a turkey shouldn't buy a partridge.

But, as to life as a whole a hundred years ago: how does it compare with the life we lead now? It is an extremely difficult question. In the first place, it was undoubtedly much dirtier. There were no bath-rooms, and few baths: we had not yet taken to washing seriously. We did not believe in fresh air: the heat of summer; and nobody thought of sleeping with his windows open. Night air was considered poisonous: besides, in London, sleep would have been impossible, for the noise of the horses' hoofs beating on the cobblestones swelled into a roar.

In the main thoroughfares, when one man met another and desired to talk to him, two went into a shop and shut the door, and shut out to some degree the terrific rattle of the streets. And so at night, all windows were shut, and if it were chilly weather, a warming pan was run between the sheets—a practice I heard highly commended by a London specialist a few years ago.

And if the sleeper were a man of substance, he laid himself to rest in a fourpost bedstead, and drew the curtains all about it. He covered his head with a nightcap, and put his watch in a pocket in the drapery above his pillow. And if he woke up, he would draw the curtain aside and see the time by the dim rushlight burning behind a shade in the hearth. Matches—in the modern sense—were just being discovered; but they were a curiosity, not an article of common use.

A dirty, stuffy time, if you like; but also a jolly time. There were no "hours," either for sweets, tobacco, strong drink, or anything else. If you wanted a cigar and brandy and water warm, at four o'clock in the morning, you could have both, without seeking far. If you were fond of the theatre, you could enjoy about six hours of it in the pit for your two shillings. A tragedy or melodrama, a farce and after-piece: good value for your money.

Many people preferred to go in after nine at half-price, and then there was supper afterwards, beginning at midnight, and going on to any hour you please. That arrangement gave a man time to dine in comfort at the tavern—a huge beefsteak and a bottle of port made the meal, very likely—and then go on to the play.

There was one modern theatrical touch about the year 1827. Miss Gradden, of the Lane—did her name suggest, I wonder, the useful Mrs. Grusden, of the Crummles company?—was taken out of her part and refused to resume it at an emergency without due rehearsal. Whereupon Mr. Wallack, the stage manager—afterwards founder of Wallack's Theatre, New York?—fined Miss Gradden three weeks' salary. The lady sued and recovered, I am glad to say. She was earning £10 a week; about £40, I suppose, in our money.

In one respect, the London of 1827 was a very horrible and awful London. On certain set days, a man with a tender heart would not walk near the Holborn end of the Old Bailey. He might hear a rattle and a crack as the New Drop fell, and see half a dozen men swinging in the air. In 1827 men were being hanged for arson, coining false money, trunk stealing, forgery, burglary. Sometimes there were hideous scenes on the scaffold. One man, hearing the first creak of the mechanism, leapt clear of the deadly platform on to the firm boards, and so hung slant-wise over the pit, till the executioner thrust him down to destruction by main force.

And here is a great distinction: The London of 1827 was a tiny place—though Cobbett called it the Wen—compared with our huge town. Little Dorrit walked easily into the fields from the Marshalsea; northward, London ended at the Angel, Islington. Outside this circle, there were villages, hamlets, small county towns. You might live in Putney all your days and never go to London.

In 1827 the Peckham and Dulwich farmers suffered grievous loss from a sheepdog who had turned "rogue" and ravaged their folds. It will be remembered that certain immortals, taking tea at the Spaniards, Hampstead, were agreed that they were in the country, as, indeed, they were.

Which reminds me: that pleasant tea-party at Hampstead ended, and for Mrs. Bardell, in the Fleet Prison. "The Debtors" prisons were, no doubt, very dreadful places; and yet men were jolly in them. In '27 the prisoners of the King's Bench had a mock parliamentary election, and were as merry as may be—till the Marshal ended their mirth with the harshest severity.

In some respects, a horrible time, this year 1827. And yet:—

Progress, no doubt, has been immense: but can our age show anything comparable with the *caritas*, the genial good humor and friendliness of "Pickwick"?

Arthur Machen
Selected Works

FICTION

Novels

The Three Impostors (1895)

Hill of Dreams (1907)

The Terror (1917)

The Secret Glory (1922)

The Green Round (1933)

Novellas

The Great God Pan (1894) Includes *The Inmost Light.*

House of Souls (1906) Collection which includes *A Fragment of Life* and
The White People.

The Great Return (1915)

Short Story Collections

*The Angel of Mons: The Bowmen
and Other Legends of the War* (1915)

Ornaments in Jade (1924)

The Shining Pyramid (1925)

The Cosy Room (1936)

The Children of the Pool (1936)

Other Fiction

Eleusinia (1881) Poetry.

The Anatomy of Tobacco (1884)

The Chronicle of Clemendy (1888)

NONFICTION

Memoirs

Far Off Things (1922)

Things Near and Far (1923)

The London Adventure (1924)

Essays

Strange Roads (1923)

Dog and Duck (1924)

Dreads and Drolls (1926)

Notes and Queries (1926)

Tom O'Bedlam and His Song (1930)

Bridles and Spurs (1951)

Mist and Mystery (2022)

Miscellaneous Nonfiction

Hieroglyphics (1902) Literary criticism.

The House of the Hidden Light (1904) With A. E. Waite.

Dr. Stiggins, His Views and Principles (1906) Religious criticism.

War and the Christian Faith (1918) Christian apologetics.

Precious Balms (1926) Literary criticism.

The Canning Wonder (1925) Historical criticism.

A Reader of Curious Books (2020) Literary and antiquarian criticism.

What Do We Know? (2023)

Translations

The Heptameron (1886)

The Way to Attain (1889)

The Memoirs of Casanova (1894)

Casanova's Escape (1925)

Remarks Upon Hermodactylus (1933)

References

Goldstone, Adrian & Sweester, Wesley D. *Bibliography of Arthur Machen* (University of Texas Press, 1965).

Machen, Arthur. *A Few Letters* (Cleveland; The Rowfant Club, 1932).

Reynolds, Aiden & Charlton, William. *Arthur Machen* (London; The Richards Press, 1963).

Van Patten, Nathan. *There Are Some Who Mourn.* (Canton; Privately printed, 1948).

Other Books by Arthur Machen

The Great Return, Annotated Edition: Includes the classic novella, *The Sangraal, Parts I-III*, new essays and appreciations.

A Reader of Curious Books: A collection of rare material previously unavailable since its original 1887 publication in the *Walford's Antiquarian Magazine*.

Mist and Mystery: Recovered stories and essays by Arthur Machen from the pages of *T. P.'s Weekly*.

What Do We Know?: An exploration into the strange and unusual, collected from Arthur Machen's column in the pages of *The Observer*.

Dreamt in Fire, The Expanded Second Edition: An original collection of Machen's fiction and essays which provides a comprehensive survey of his work.

A Secret Language: A miniature manifesto by Machen on his approach to literature and Christian mysticism. Annotated.

Levavi Oculos: The brilliant short story which highlights an application of Machen's literary theory. Annotated.